THE FIRST LETTER OF

PETER

KEN FLEMING

LUKE 24:27

Developed as a study course by Emmaus Correspondence School, founded in 1942.

Many Bible study courses may also be taken via smart phones, tablets, and computers. For more information, visit the ECS website www.ecsministries.org.

The First Letter of Peter

Ken Fleming

Published by:
Emmaus Correspondence School
(A division of ECS Ministries)
PO Box 1028
Dubuque, IA 52004-1028
phone: (563) 585-2070
email: ecsorders@ecsministries.org
website: www.ecsministries.org

First Edition 2008 (AK '08), 2 UNITS
Reprinted 2010 (AK '08), 2 UNITS
Reprinted 2015 (AK '08), 2 UNITS
Reprinted 2019 (AK '08), 2 UNITS

ISBN 978-1-59387-093-5

Code: 1PET

Copyright © 2008 ECS Ministries

Printed in the United States of America

STUDENT INSTRUCTIONS

Peter was the most prominent of the twelve disciples of the Lord Jesus Christ. He became the main spokesman for the early church in Jerusalem but later traveled among the early churches, including some that the apostle Paul had established.

At the time Peter was writing, persecution against Christians was increasing and they were under pressure to deny their new faith. In this letter (the first of two written by Peter that are part of the Bible), Peter wrote to encourage believers now living in the five provinces of Asia Minor to remember that they were pilgrims traveling toward heaven and just temporary residents in this world. His letter is full of practical instruction on attitudes and behavior to strengthen their faith and witness. The world has always been (and will continue to be) hostile to Jesus Christ and His followers. In light of that, the letter of 1 Peter contains both relevant and needed teaching and encouragement for Christians today.

Lessons You Will Study

Course Components

This course has two parts: this study course and the exam booklet.

How To Study

This study has eight chapters, and each chapter has its own exam. Begin by asking God to help you understand the material. Read the chapter through at least twice, once to get a general idea of its contents and then again, slowly, looking up any Bible references given.

Begin studying immediately, or if you are in a group, as soon as the group begins. We suggest that you keep a regular schedule by trying to complete at least one chapter per week.

Exams

In the exam booklet there is one exam for each chapter (exam 1 covers chapter 1 of the course). Do not answer the questions by what you think or have always believed. The questions are designed to find out if you understand the material given in the course.

After you have completed each chapter, review the related exam and see how well you know the answers. If you find that you are having difficulty answering the questions, review the material until you think you can answer the questions. It is important that you read the Bible passages referenced as some questions may be based on the Bible text.

How Your Exams Are Graded

Your instructor will mark any incorrectly answered questions. You will be referred back to the place in the course where the correct answer is to be found. After finishing this course with a passing average, you will be awarded a certificate.

If you enrolled in a class, submit your exam papers to the leader or secretary of the class who will send them for the entire group to the Correspondence School.

See the back of the exam booklet for more information on returning the exams for grading.

1

INTRODUCTION TO 1 PETER

The Pilgrim in a Hostile World

First Peter is a letter written by the apostle Peter to believers who were living under an increasing threat of persecution for their faith in Jesus Christ. As it is included in our Bibles we can trust it to be a message from God, inspired by the Holy Spirit, and relevant to us today. It is about living out a triumphant faith in a hostile world. It is written to pilgrims who are on their way to a better country—heaven. It is written to Christian believers in an unbelieving world where they find life difficult because they no longer belong there; they have become strangers to it. This letter is written to you and me.

The Historical Background

In the first century AD, pressure was building against the early Christians throughout the Roman Empire. The area in which Peter's readers now lived was Asia Minor (present-day Turkey). The world around them was becoming increasingly hostile to Christianity. It was in this area that evangelists Paul and Barnabas had been put out of several towns—and even stoned—by a Jewish element that was upset by the message they proclaimed, that Jesus *was* the Messiah (Acts 13-14). And in one example of Gentile hostility, heathen business interests in the province of Asia felt threatened by the Christian message and started a riot (Acts 19).

By the early sixties, the effect of the Christian gospel was turning whole communities against believers. Jewish communities were upset by its message that included teaching on freedom from the Law of Moses in light of free salvation through faith in Christ's substitutionary death. Idol worshipers were upset by the Christians' insistence that there was only one God and only one Way to Him, Jesus Christ. A decadent society was becoming aggressively hostile to Christianity's high moral standards by which it was condemned. The Roman Caesars were increasingly disturbed that Christians would not offer incense to them or worship them as gods. The first century world was hardening its heart to God's grace.

We can, to some degree, identify with the believers to whom Peter wrote this letter. We, too, sometimes have to endure this kind of pressure, where true Christians face opposition from both religious and secular interests. In many parts of the world, Christians are suffering material hardship, social estrangement, imprisonment, and even loss of life for their faith. Peter's letter gives practical guidelines on how to live as a Christian in a hostile world. It helps us to face the trials that result from declaring public allegiance to the Lord Jesus Christ. We look back to Him in His suffering and can understand our own. We then look forward to rejoicing at being with Him in His glorified state and we understand that this is the purpose of God in history. The trial of our faith leads us eventually to triumph in Christ. To embattled believers in every age, this first century letter is a priceless treasure.

Peter, One of the Twelve Disciples

More than thirty years had elapsed since Peter experienced firsthand being a disciple of the Lord Jesus Christ. Peter (originally named Simon, but renamed Peter by Jesus) was a fisherman by trade. His home was in Capernaum on the Sea of Galilee and he was in business with his brother Andrew. Andrew was, like Peter, called by Jesus to be a "fisher of men" (Matt. 4:18-19).

For three years, Peter accompanied Jesus in His witness and ministry to the Jewish people in Judea and Galilee. A reading of the four Gospels will show that Peter was the most prominent of the twelve disciples. It was Peter who, along with James and John, made up the "inner circle" of the disciples chosen by the Lord to witness certain healings and significant events, including the transfiguration and Christ's agony in Gethsemane (Mark 5:37; Matt. 17:1-8; 26:37). It was Peter who appears to have recognized Christ's deity at an early point, prompting him to confess his own sinful state (Luke 5:3-8). It was Peter who walked on the stormy lake, only to sink when he took his eyes off Jesus (Matt. 14:27-31).

It was Peter who had verbally confessed that Jesus was the Christ, the Son of God (Matt. 16:16). It was to Peter that Jesus replied that the church was to be founded on the "rock-solid" truth which Peter had just confessed. It was to Peter that the keys of the kingdom of heaven were given (Matt. 16:18-19). And yet it was Peter who thought that it was enough to forgive a person just seven times (Matt. 18:21); who refused, at first, to let Jesus wash his feet (John 13:8); and who rashly promised to never forsake Jesus but then openly denied even knowing Him when challenged (Matt. 26:33, 69-75).

Over the course of Jesus' public ministry Peter would have witnessed the steady rise in hostility toward Him among the Jewish religious leaders. The nation of Israel followed their leaders in rejecting Jesus as their Messiah. They condemned Him to die a criminal's death by means of crucifixion in Jerusalem. Peter witnessed it all. But it was Peter's joy and consolation to not only see the empty tomb but to have been visited by the risen Christ Himself (Luke 24:34). Peter was now forgiven for denying Him and restored to fellowship with His Savior and Lord. It was Peter that the risen Christ charged with "feeding" His sheep after His ascension to heaven (John 21:15-17).

Peter, the Apostle

Peter used one of the "keys" of the kingdom on the day of Pentecost when, in the power of the Holy Spirit, he boldly preached that Jesus' resurrection proved He *was* Israel's promised Messiah (the Christ). As a result, 3,000 Jews repented of crucifying Him and were forgiven and saved (Acts 2:1-38). From the book of Acts chapters 2 through 12 we learn that Peter became the main spokesman for the early church in Jerusalem. In these chapters we see Peter preaching the gospel (particularly Christ's resurrection), performing healing miracles, standing up courageously against threats from the Jewish leaders, suffering physical abuse for his stand for Christ, and disciplining sinning believers. We even see him being imprisoned and then being freed by an angel!

It was Peter's privilege to use the second of God's "keys" when he introduced the gospel to the Gentiles through a man named Cornelius. When he and other Gentiles believed Peter's message that Jesus was the Messiah of Old Testament prophecies, God poured out His Spirit in a second Pentecost-like experience. It was Peter who reported this significant event to the church's leaders in Jerusalem. They trusted his account of it as evidence that God was, by His grace, now saving Gentiles through their personal faith in Christ, just as He was saving Jews (Acts 10:1-11:18).

Later, when the apostle Paul brought Titus, the converted Gentile, to Jerusalem, it was Peter who gave them "the right hand of fellowship" (Gal. 2:1-9). It was also Peter who visited the first Gentile church in Antioch and affirmed the gospel as preached by Paul and Barnabas (Gal. 2:10-14). Finally, at the Jerusalem Council, it was Peter who again plainly stated that, by God's grace, salvation was freely available to both Jews and Gentiles (Acts 15:1-21). That was about the year AD 40. Peter had faithfully and effectively used "the keys of the kingdom" that the Lord had entrusted to him.

Peter's Later Life

From that point on, the New Testament provides only a few hints about Peter's life. He probably did not stay in Jerusalem; we do not see his name mentioned in later New Testament references to the church there. He may well have become an itinerant (traveling) missionary to people of Jewish background, very much as Paul did to those who were Gentiles (Gal. 2:9). It appears that he was married and that his wife traveled with him (Matt. 8:14; 1 Cor. 9:5). He seems to have visited the church in Corinth, where one of the divisive elements was a group that boasted of Peter as their leader (1 Cor. 1:12; 3:21-22).

It is probable that Peter had at least visited churches in the five provinces of Asia Minor mentioned that he is writing to, that is, Pontus, Bithynia, Asia, Galatia, and Cappadocia (1 Pet. 1:1). It will be helpful to the student to look at a map at this point (usually found in the back of most Bibles). There was plenty of time—nearly twenty-five years—for him to work extensively in a large area like this.

Peter is also associated with the city of Babylon, from which he wrote this letter (1 Pet. 5:13). He was evidently in Rome at the end of his life. The Bible does not mention this, but from statements made by Clement of Rome writing in the year AD 96, it appears that Peter died in Rome under the persecution of Nero about the year 67. *Unger's Bible Dictionary* takes the view that Peter did not arrive there until the year of his death, which seems to best fit the evidence we have. Tradition has it that he was condemned to die by crucifixion, the same death suffered by Jesus Himself. He asked, however, to be crucified upside down, as he did not count himself worthy to suffer exactly the same kind of death as his Lord.

The People to Whom Peter Wrote

The readers of 1 Peter lived in the five provinces already named. Three of these are mentioned in the New Testament in connection with the apostle Paul. Paul planted four churches in Galatia on his first missionary journey (Acts 13:14-14:23). On his second journey, Paul had expressed a plan to go to Bithynia, but he was refused permission to do so by the Holy Spirit (Acts 16:7). Paul planted the large church at Ephesus in Asia on his third missionary journey (Acts 19:1-20:1). Peter probably evangelized further north than the Galatian and Asian cities where Paul worked.

Peter wrote to established churches that were under the care of elders (5:1). He was probably not the first evangelist among them, as he refers to "those who preached the gospel to you" (1:12). But the epistle (letter) does imply that Peter had worked among them and that, in writing, he was carrying out the instructions of the Lord Jesus to feed His sheep (John 21:15-17).

The believers to whom Peter wrote included both slaves (2:18-21) and free citizens (2:16). Some of them had been Gentile idolaters, for he described them as having been "called out of darkness into His marvelous light" (2:9). They had been delivered from heathen practices such as "abominable idolatries" (4:3-4). It is likely that some were from a Jewish background as Peter quotes freely from the Old Testament, with which they would have been familiar. Peter sums up his readers' identity when he closes the letter with a benediction of peace "to . . . all who are in Christ Jesus" (5:14). Whatever their ethnic roots or social standing were, they were one in Christ. We who read and study this letter today are included.

The Place of Origin and the Date of Writing

The identity of Babylon from which Peter was writing has been widely debated (5:13). Many commentators have assumed that Peter was in Rome when he wrote 1 Peter and that the word Babylon is a cryptic reference to it. However, there is no firm evidence that Peter was in Rome before the year of his death. It seems better to understand Babylon as naturally referring to the well-known city by that name on the River Euphrates. Peter probably went there to minister to believers. These people may have had some previous contact with those to whom Peter wrote, as they sent their greetings to them.

The date of writing was almost certainly before the persecution under Nero in the year AD 67 because there is no mention of martyrs. Peter, however, does see impending trouble for believers. He speaks of "those who revile your good conduct" and those who are "speaking evil of you" (3:9, 16; 4:4). In view of the increasing pressure, a date of AD 64 seems reasonable. At this time, Paul was still in prison in Rome and had just written the Prison Epistles (Ephesians, Philippians, Colossians, and Philemon).

The Theme and Purpose of This Letter

First Peter is valuable to us as a kind of handbook for pilgrims living in a foreign land. As believers we are sojourners (temporary resident aliens) in the world, a world that is passing away (1 John 2:17). Our true home is in heaven, toward which we are progressing (Phil. 3:20). That makes us pilgrims moving toward a new and better land. Here, we can expect trials and suffering. There, we anticipate participating in the glory of God's Son (Rom. 8:15-18). Peter encourages us to see the trials in the red glow of the sufferings of Christ and in the radiant light of the glory of Christ. *Suffering* and *glory* are recurring themes in this letter.

2

THE PILGRIM'S WONDERFUL SALVATION (1:1-12)

In the first part of 1 Peter chapter 1 we will learn why a good understanding of our salvation helps us live a joyful life in a hostile world. We will learn two great truths about God's role in our salvation: (1) He has chosen us, and (2) He has given us new life (caused us to be born again spiritually). Then we will learn about two effects that salvation has on us. First, it enables us to rejoice even in trials, because we now have the perspective that in the future we shall see the Lord Jesus Christ fully revealed in His glory. Second, as a result of now being enlightened by the indwelling Holy Spirit, we understand the prophetic statements in the Old Testament about both the suffering and the glory of the Lord Jesus Christ. These truths strengthen us as pilgrims on our journey.

Peter Greets His Readers (1:1)

Peter greets his readers in the customary way of his day. He identifies himself with the name Jesus gave him when he first became a disciple. "'You are Simon . . . You shall be called Cephas [Peter],' (which is translated, A Stone)" (John 1:42). By the grace of God, Peter's character changed over time as well. We too are to grow spiritually to reflect more and more our new name of "Christian" which, although originally coined by their opponents (Acts 11:26), is a fitting term, as it means "belonging to Christ."

Peter's authority for writing to these Christians is that he is "an apostle of Jesus Christ." Apostles were a specific group of men who had been with the Lord during His ministry on earth, had seen Him after His resurrection, and were specially chosen and gifted by God to establish the church (Acts

1:22-24; 1 Cor. 12:28). (The apostle Paul was an exception to the first of these qualifications as he was not one of Christ's original twelve disciples. He was uniquely chosen by God to be His apostle to the Gentiles.) As an apostle of the Lord Jesus, Peter spoke and wrote by the authority Christ had given him and under the inspiration of the Holy Spirit. The Christians reading this letter would have recognized that they needed to pay attention to whatever Peter wrote and act on it.

Peter termed the recipients of this letter "pilgrims of the Dispersion," and later, "sojourners and pilgrims" (v. 1; 2:11). This description of believers in the world sets the tone for the whole letter. As believers we have been "delivered . . . from the power of darkness and conveyed . . . into the kingdom of the Son of His love" (Col. 1:13). We are sojourners (temporary resident aliens) in the sense that this world is no longer "home" to us; we do not belong here because this world is hostile to the Lord Jesus and His kingdom (John 18:36). But we are not only temporary residents here; we are also pilgrims on the way to where we *do* belong: a "heavenly country" (Heb. 11:16). It is important for believers today, as it was for Peter's readers, to grasp the concept of being sojourners in this world and pilgrims to the next. It helps us to keep a loose hold on things that relate to this life and to separate ourselves from worldly influences. It also gives us purpose for how we conduct our lives here so that we do not just "bide our time" till we go home to heaven.

Peter's readers were scattered ("of the Dispersion") throughout five Roman provinces. The scattering of early Christians was caused by persecution, first by jealous Jews and later by the Gentiles. Although this must have caused emotional distress and material hardship, everywhere they went they spread their faith (Acts 8:2-4). Today God has His people scattered over all five continents, and often they feel lonely and discouraged. If you are one of these you will find encouragement from this letter of Peter's.

Scattered as they were throughout these Roman provinces, Peter immediately reminds them that their situation was no accident of history. They had been chosen by a sovereign God for His purposes. The two words "elect" and "pilgrims" belong together. God's choice related to their eternal salvation and their earthly situation. Peter describes three wonderful aspects of God's choice of them (v. 2).

The Triune God Has Provided Salvation (1:2)

Christians are chosen "according to the foreknowledge of God the Father." His foreknowledge relates to His particular regard and love for us before the world was created (Eph. 1:4). We can only understand it as the outworking of the grace of God the Father. It is more than simply God knowing in advance that we would believe the gospel. By the term "foreknowledge" we understand that, in eternity past, God centered His attention on us and chose (elected) all those on whom He graciously focused His attention. Election is a wonderful truth for believers. It should both comfort our hearts and cause us to praise God for His kindness.

We are chosen "in sanctification of the Spirit." The Holy Spirit sets us apart to be saved and to serve. The Spirit puts God's choice and purpose into effect (2 Thess. 2:13; Rom. 8:9-10). We are chosen "for obedience," referring primarily to the outcome of God's present work in His people. God's chosen people ought to be constantly growing in obedience to the truth after they are saved (1 Peter 1:14, 22). Obedience here probably also includes the initial "obedience to the faith" in Christ as Savior (Rom. 1:5; 16:26).

Peter then speaks of the "sprinkling" by the blood of Jesus Christ. In the context, it seems the best way to interpret this phrase is to link it to the Old Testament practice of sprinkling sacrificial blood on the diseased leper who, having been healed, was ceremonially cleansed and restored to fellowship with God's people (Lev. 14:1-9). David also used this symbolism in his prayer for forgiveness: "Purge me with hyssop [the branch used to sprinkle the sacrificial blood] and I shall be clean" (Ps. 51:7). Believers in Christ are blessed with forgiveness of all our sins in the judicial sense (affecting our standing and position) and with forgiveness for daily sins in a relational sense (affecting our relationship to the heavenly Father while here on earth) when we confess them. By using the term "sprinkling of the blood" Peter reminds them that every time their fellowship with God is disrupted by disobedience they can be assured of restoration and cleansing on the basis of Christ's atoning work. When they confess their sins God forgives them because "the blood of Jesus Christ His Son cleanses [keeps on cleansing] us from all sin" (1 John 1:7-9).

Peter completes his greeting statement with the prayer that grace and peace be theirs in fullest measure. Paul used this prayer for grace and peace in eleven of his letters. Grace is a word that summarizes God's favor bestowed on guilty man. Peace is the state of well-being that results from being saved by God's grace.

We can summarize this section by noting how each of the Persons of the Trinity is involved in effecting our salvation. God the Father favorably regarded us from before the foundation of the world. God the Spirit is sanctifying us to be like the Lord Jesus Christ. God the Son is leading us to obedience and providing His cleansing blood when we fail. No wonder Peter bursts forth in a doxology of praise in the next section!

The Nature of Our Salvation (1:3-5)

In the first two verses we learned what God has done and is doing for believers. Now Peter goes on to describe salvation in the future. As pilgrims, the hope of coming glory inspires us to move forward. It is called a living hope.

The section begins with an expression of praise to God for who He is. "Blessed be the God and Father of our Lord Jesus Christ." How often, though, we think only of the gifts and neglect the Giver! Peter addresses God as the "Father of our Lord Jesus Christ" reminding us that, in the Godhead, the Father and the Son act consistently within their roles: God, as Father, directs and administers and Christ, as Son, responds and obeys. For example, "The Father has sent the Son as Savior of the world" (1 John 4:14). "The Father of our Lord Jesus Christ" deserves our praise.

After the praise for who God is, there is praise for what God does in giving us "a living hope" (v. 3). It begins with His "abundant mercy" which is His compassion poured out on us in our helpless condition. According to His mercy He has caused us to be "born again." In speaking of the new birth, perhaps Peter was recalling Jesus' conversation with Nicodemus (John 3:1-21).

We are born again to a "living hope"—the confident expectation we have while living in this hostile world that God will fulfill all His promises regarding our future. *Hope* as used in the New Testament is not just a possible outcome. It is always certain, because it is based on the trustworthy promises of God. Hope abides (remains) as a vital spiritual experience for the Christian, like faith and love (1 Cor. 13:13). It is "living" because it has the capacity to constantly become more real to us. Like the "new birth" from which it springs, it is secured by the resurrection of Jesus Christ from the dead (v. 3).

The substance of our "living hope" is described as an "inheritance" (v. 4). Having been born again as children of God, we are made heirs. Our inheritance does not relate to life on earth, like the inheritance of the land of Canaan that God gave to the Israelites (Num. 26:53-56). In view of the fact that Christians are pilgrims and sojourners on this earth, our inheritance is in heaven with Christ in God's own presence.

Our inheritance in heaven is so wonderful that Peter can only describe it by what it is *not* (v. 4). It is "incorruptible," in that it cannot wear out. It is "undefiled," in that it cannot spoil. It "does not fade," in that it cannot diminish in quality. Nothing on earth, including the earth itself, compares to it. And it is absolutely secure, for God has it "reserved in heaven for [us]."

As pilgrims on earth we should be encouraged by this living hope that God has blessed us with. Our hearts are assured of its reality because while we live here we are "kept by the power of God" (v. 5). This is God's responsibility. *Our* responsibility is to continually exercise faith in God's power to save us. Genuine faith perseveres; it does not fail. The topic of faith is a major emphasis for pilgrims in this chapter (vv. 5, 7, 9, 21). In exercising faith we remain constantly aware that God is keeping (protecting) us until our salvation is brought to completion.

The completed "salvation ready to be revealed in the last time" refers to a future time when all that has been planned and guaranteed by the work of Christ will be realized (v. 5). It will be when the Lord Jesus Christ will be fully revealed (unveiled) with all His saints before a watching world. We can understand salvation as relating to the past, the present, and the future. We *have been saved* from the *penalty* of sin (Eph. 2:8-9); we *are being saved* from the *power* of sin (Rom. 5:10); we *will be saved* from the *presence* of sin, which will begin when we are caught up to be with the Lord (Heb. 9:28). Peter has the future aspect of salvation in view in verse 5.

In summary, our "living hope" is guaranteed by the resurrection of Christ, and because He is the "firstfruits" of those to be raised from the dead (1 Cor. 15:23), He has secured a wonderful inheritance for God's children that we will experience and enjoy at the final stage of our salvation.

The Relation of Trials to Salvation (1:6-7)

The "living hope," which obviously relates to the future, gives us cause for joy in our present circumstances (v. 6). The phrase "In this" refers to everything that has been promised in the previous three verses. It includes the new birth, our inheritance in heaven, the protecting power of God, and the anticipation of complete salvation. So "in this" we are to "greatly rejoice," knowing the promises are sure. Peter views rejoicing in the coming glory as normal Christian experience and exercise, even when present circumstances are hard. Peter observed that some of his readers where being distressed by various trials, but that they have been rejoicing in the hope of their future deliverance, not just tolerating their trials. These first century Christians show us by example that true joy is not affected by external circumstances.

Trials are necessary (v. 6). Many of us do not "greatly rejoice" under the pressure of trials. Instead, we grumble. The words "if need be" show us that trials are sometimes needed to mature us (Heb. 12:10-11). Trials are part of God's training program for pilgrims. The phrase "a little while" reminds us that, by comparison to our future blessing, trials are short-term and temporary (2 Cor. 4:17-18).

Trials have a specific purpose (v. 7). They reveal the genuineness of faith, which will one day be "found to praise, honor, and glory at the revelation of Jesus Christ" (v. 7). The "genuineness" of their faith does not refer to the truthfulness of the message they believed but to the reality of their response. Their faith, as they lived it every day, would prove triumphant in the test and would result in praise from the Lord at His revelation. His "revelation" refers to the *public* phase of His second coming, when He will be openly made known to the world accompanied by His saints (not His coming to take the church to be with Him [1 Thess. 4:16-17]).

Peter uses the imagery of gold being refined by extreme heat to illustrate believers' faith being tested by trials. Impurities are removed from the gold in the refining process, after which the gold is ready to be used. Genuine faith which has been "refined . . . in the furnace of affliction [trials]" is said to be "more . . . desired . . . than gold" (compare Psalm 19:10; Isaiah 48:10). God values His people more than gold. He values man's trust in Himself above everything else. So at His public appearing, the Lord Jesus Christ will publicly recognize those who have demonstrated faith in Him in the trials they have endured.

Believers whose faith proves genuine when tried will be given a threefold heavenly commendation (v. 7). The *praise* relates to God's approval and public commendation: "Well done, good and faithful servant" (Matt. 25:21; 1 Cor. 4:5). The *glory* has to do with the saints' participation in the glory of the future life with Christ (Rom. 8:17) and being changed into His likeness (Phil. 3:21). *Honor* will be the reward for tested faith when the Lord will honor those before the world which has despised them (John 12:26). And whatever we saints are commended for at this time will also add to Christ's own glory!

Responses to Salvation (1:8-9)

Peter commends these suffering believers for loving Christ even though they had never seen Him or known Him personally (unlike Peter himself). The Lord Jesus Christ was the focus of their love and faith. Their love for Him was in response to His love for them (1 John 4:19). Biblical love is not an emotion. Loving God shows itself in such things as praising, pleasing, and obeying God. The second response to Christ was to believe in Him. Peter was there on the day of resurrection when Thomas had demanded to see the Lord before he would believe He had risen from the dead. Perhaps Peter was thinking of Jesus' answer to Thomas: "Blessed are those who have not seen and yet have believed" (John 20:29). To believe in Christ is to continually and confidently trust Him.

As a result of loving Christ and believing in Him these believers "greatly rejoice with joy inexpressible and full of glory." The phrase "greatly rejoice" was used in verse 6, but here Peter adds the words, "with an inexpressible and glorious joy." In verse 6 the cause for rejoicing was hope about the future. Here, the cause for rejoicing is personal love for Christ. It is inexpressible and glorious—so wonderful that it is beyond the power of words to express. We experience this joy when Christ is the focus of our life. We lose it when the things of earth are our focus.

Peter goes on to say that in the process of believing in Christ and rejoicing in Him, these believers were "receiving . . . the salvation of [their] souls" (v. 9). Salvation here refers, as in verse 5, to the full possession of all its benefits. There is a sense, though, in which we can *anticipate* our future blessing, entering into the enjoyment of it just as if it were already ours. The "end" of our faith means its goal, or consummation, not its conclusion. The spiritual joy of our salvation is something we should experience on an ongoing basis (Isa. 12:2-3).

Privileges of Salvation (1:10-12)

Peter concludes his thoughts on what we are terming *The Pilgrim's Wonderful Salvation* by reminding his readers that they are more privileged than the Old Testament prophets. These servants of God often spoke and wrote of the coming Savior and the eternal blessing He would bring when "they spoke of the grace that was to come to you" (v. 10). In this context, Peter uses the word "grace" to define salvation as the undeserved favor of God. In Acts 20:24 it is called the "gospel of the grace of God."

Although the Old Testament prophets wrote of this grace, they did not fully understand what they were writing (compare Daniel 12:8). In their strong desire to understand it, they "made careful search and inquiry, seeking to know" (vv. 10-11). They searched the Scriptures diligently (see John 5:39, where the same word "search" is used). What they wanted to know was the "person or time the Spirit of Christ was indicating as He predicted the sufferings of Christ and the glories that would follow." They searched for the identity of Messiah about whom they wrote. They wanted to understand His sufferings and glory. How would both be fulfilled, and when? Would it happen in their lifetimes or in the future?

The reason they did not fully understand their own writings was that they wrote under the inspiration of the Holy Spirit and not always from their own knowledge or experience. The title "the Spirit of Christ" shows that the Spirit's central purpose in inspiring the prophets was to predict the coming of the Christ (Messiah). He predicted, for example, the Messiah's sufferings, as in Psalm 22 and Isaiah 53. He also predicted the "glories that would follow" those sufferings. These glories include His resurrection, His revelation to the whole world, and His rule as King. Psalm 24 and Isaiah 11 are two of many Old Testament passages that speak of His future glory.

The fact that Messiah would suffer first and afterward receive glory would have encouraged the believers to whom Peter was writing because *they* were suffering for their allegiance in Him. We too should "consider Him who endured such hostility" so that we should not "become weary and discouraged" (Heb. 12:3). But they were also looking forward to "praise, honor, and glory" when Jesus Christ will be revealed.

There is another form of encouragement for Peter's readers in verse 12: they were privileged to understand God's wonderful salvation better than either the prophets or the angels. God had revealed to the prophets that when they wrote of the sufferings and glories of the Messiah, they were not serving themselves but believers who would live after Messiah came. What had been a mystery to the prophets was the revealed gospel that had been preached to these people now living in Asia Minor, for instance. The prophets did not understand that there would be a long period between the suffering and the final glory of Messiah. Even Peter himself did not understand it when Jesus revealed it to the disciples (Matt. 16:21-23). After the resurrection, however, Christ again taught them and they all understood (Luke 24:45-46). And later Peter himself preached, "Those things which God foretold by the mouth of all His prophets, that the Christ would suffer, He has thus fulfilled" (Acts 3:18).

Like us today, these scattered believers could now understand the prophecies and believe the gospel. Even angels desire to look into (literally, "to gain a clear glimpse of") the "things" concerning Christ's sufferings and glories. Their holy curiosity is turning to fuller understanding. Peter's pilgrim readers, like us today, would be encouraged that even angels are interested in the unfolding drama of salvation's history.

3

THE PILGRIM'S HOLY BEHAVIOR (1:13-25)

In this passage we learn that being saved should result in a changed lifestyle. Peter has told us that we are "born again" into God's family as His children (v. 3). Building on our relationship with God as children he stresses that our behavior should not be like those in this world. The first difference relates to ourselves; the second, to God; the third, to man: (1) a holy lifestyle (vv. 13-16); (2) reverence for God (vv. 17-21); (3) love for one another (vv. 22-25).

The Mindset of the Christian (1:13)

When Peter begins with "therefore" he is referring back to the blessings of salvation mentioned in verses 3-12, specifically that God chose us in eternity past, gives us a secure hope for eternity future, and grants us spiritual blessings to enjoy in the temporary present. "Therefore" we are to live today in a manner consistent with our past calling and our future hope. This new lifestyle does not come naturally to us. We must actively pursue it (Gal. 5:16). The pursuit of holy living begins in our minds, and verse 13 tells us of three major adjustments to be made in our thinking.

1. Mental discipline. "Gird up the loins of your mind." We should not miss the biblical imagery here. It refers to the long robes that men wore in Peter's day. When doing active work or when running, they would tuck the robes up and tie them around the waist with a sash, sometimes called a belt or girdle. The words "gird up" come from the word "girdle." The word "loins" refers to the waist. "Girding up the loins" therefore meant to be prepared for action.

Peter is telling us here that the activity of holy living requires a mindset focused on God and His Word (Eph. 6:14). Many believers allow their minds, like loosely flowing robes, to be undisciplined and unfocused. They are unprepared for the demands of a pilgrim life because they do not see the present in the light of the future. We are, Peter says, to consciously gird up the loins of our minds—to focus and discipline our thinking on eternal realities. Only in this way will we keep our minds free of unnecessary and unprofitable things and be ready to assess the situation for God's glory.

2. Mental sobriety. The second command is "Be sober." In this context, sobriety does not refer to abstaining from alcohol but from mental intoxication from stimulants in the world (compare Romans 12:2). Peter uses the same word twice more in this letter (4:7; 5:8). Being sober in the mind is to be clear thinking, able to concentrate on the task. We must be able to evaluate things correctly so that we are not thrown off balance by every new and fascinating idea.

The clear-thinking Christian pilgrim has a mind that sees the world from a biblical perspective. This is called "having a biblical worldview." He is not swayed by reasoning that leaves God out of the picture. He sees that "the world is passing away, and the lust of it" (1 John 2:17). He does not allow the intoxicating influence of the passing world to blur his spiritual vision. He is aware of the dangers of mental intoxication possible in the overindulgence of sports, travel, business, pleasure, and many forms of entertainment.

3. Mental focus. "Rest your hope fully upon the grace that is to be brought to you at the revelation of Jesus Christ." The word "rest" means the "purposeful directing" of our hope on the coming glory. Because we confidently expect that the Lord Jesus Christ will one day be openly revealed to the whole world, we see ourselves on a path leading to His glory and our reward. Just as a prospector for gold "sets his mind" on the big nugget he hopes to find, so the pilgrim sets his mind on the grace he will receive when Christ is revealed.

The word "grace" in this verse refers to the eternal benefits in store for believers when Christ is revealed in glory. As with verse 10, Peter has in mind here the public revelation of Christ, not His coming to rapture the church, which the world will not witness. Peter had been taught many times by Jesus Himself of the coming messianic kingdom. His focus here is the glorious future when Jesus Christ will reign and when believers will reign with Him. He encourages his readers to have that perspective too.

The Lifestyle Standard for the Christian (1:14-16)

Holy living, which begins in the mind, also involves the will. We are to consciously decide to not conform to the desires that marked our life before conversion, but rather to conform to the holiness of God. First, the negative side. As "obedient children" we are no longer to be shaped by the lusts which shaped the old life. The word "conform" is only used here and in one other place in the New Testament where the context is the same: "And do not be conformed to this world . . ." (Rom. 12:2).

Just as clay conforms to the shape of a mold, so people conform to the shape of their desires. The "evil desires" of the old life can be summarized as pleasures, possessions, and power (1 John 2:15-16). Peter knew that all these desires still tempt the believer, but we are not to let them shape us as they once did. Some of the "lusts of the flesh" are listed in Galatians 5:19-21 and 1 Peter 4:2-3. The life of obedience to God is radically different. It is characterized by pleasing the Lord Jesus Christ rather than our flesh. The phrase "in your ignorance" refers to ignorance of spiritual realities before we were saved. After we are saved we become "obedient children," or better, "children of obedience," that is, people who are characterized by obedience (in this instance, to God). We must reject the old desires that formerly shaped us and not conform to the world's system.

The positive side is next. "But as He who called you is holy, you also be holy in all your conduct." This is a call to holiness. We are to be shaped by God's pure standards and reflect His holiness. The command is based first on the calling of God. This is the first of five references to *God's calling in 1 Peter* (1:15; 2:9, 21; 3:9; 5:10). God purposed us to be holy before the world began (Eph. 1:4). During our present pilgrimage we are "call[ed] . . . in holiness" (1 Thess. 4:7). Living holy lives is one of God's purposes for us.

The command is also based on God's character. The standard for our holy behavior is the absolute holiness of God Himself. "As He . . . is holy," means *because* He is holy; no Christian can achieve absolute holiness this side of heaven. Holiness is perhaps the most emphasized characteristic of God in Scripture. It shows His *set-apartness* from sin. Angelic beings surround His throne saying, "Holy, holy, holy, is the LORD of hosts: the whole earth is full of His glory" (Isa. 6:3). What a standard! As pilgrims we are commanded to strive, in the power of the indwelling Spirit, toward holiness "in all [we] do." Our lives should reflect our *desire* and *intent* to be holy. There is no room for blaming our behavior on a childhood experience or difficult background. God's own holiness is to be the measure of our present action.

Third, the command is based on the Word of God. The reason we should be holy is that Scripture says so. "Because it is written, 'Be holy, for I am holy.'" Peter quotes from Leviticus, where this command is mentioned no less than five times (11:44, 45; 19:2; 20:7, 26). Holy living is a consistent and clear command in both the Old and the New Testaments.

We have noted that the command to be holy is based on the calling of God, the character of God, and the Word of God. For us as believers, these form the basis of true ethics. Our ethics should not change with the times, the direction of our culture, or in light of the decisions of high-court judges. The pilgrim believer who maintains holy behavior in an increasingly unholy society is bound to meet opposition. We must be prepared for that!

The Motivation for Living a Holy Life (1:17)

Fear of displeasing God is the principle in these verses that should motivate us to holy living. In Old Testament times, God chose Israel as a nation to be set apart to serve and glorify Him. God called them "a holy nation" (Exod. 19:6). God gave them the Law at Mount Sinai. They agreed to keep the Law to reflect His holy standards (Exod. 24:3). The record of the remaining Old Testament shows that Israel did *not* live as a set-apart people; instead, they lived just like the heathen and worshipped heathen gods.

Peter now exhorts these New Testament people of God to reflect God's holiness in the way *they* lived. He reminds them that God is watching them (and us). God judges us fairly and out of individual and intimate knowledge of us. We should never presume that His love for us will allow any disobedience to go unnoticed. In fact, out of His love for us, He will discipline us (see Hebrews 12:5-11), but always for our good and to encourage our spiritual maturity.

The sense of verse 17 is that since we habitually call on the Father for help, we must keep in mind that He is also an impartial Judge, even of His own children. He judges and rewards us according to what we do. He has no favorites. He treats each of His children with both discipline and encouragement that are designed for our greatest good. God wants us to reflect His holiness as obedient children.

The fear of God is an unpopular concept today. But fearing God is a proper and biblical response to His holiness. It is more than simply reverence for God. We are to fear God's discipline when we sin. Thus when we are tempted to sin we know that under the discipline of a holy and just God we will reap the consequences what we sow (Gal. 6:7).

This verse reminds us that we fear God in the pilgrim context "throughout the time of [our] stay here." Even as sojourners in the world with its shifting situational ethics, we are always to fear God. The word "stay" is similar to a word in Acts 13:17 where the Israelites' "dwelling" in Egypt is described. God's people lived in exile there until God delivered them. We too are exiles in the enemy territory of this world, away from "home." Like the Israelites in Egypt, we are to maintain our fear of God.

Christ Died to Redeem Us (1:18-19)

Peter now draws our attention to several things about our redemption which should motivate us to fear God. Our eternal salvation from eternal judgment was brought about at a great cost. Redemption as a biblical truth refers to the payment of a ransom price to free us from the bondage of sin. We can understand the spiritual meaning of redemption when we understand the Roman practice of buying slaves. Occasionally wealthy citizens, for their own reasons, would buy slaves out of the market and set them free. In spiritual terms, we were slaves to sin, unable to free ourselves from sin's bondage (John 8:34). Christ paid the required ransom price, redeemed us, and set us free from the slave market of sin.

Verses 18 and 19 emphasize the tremendous cost of our redemption—Christ's precious blood. Peter compares the precious metals of international money markets to the precious blood with which we have been redeemed. When gold is compared to the price of our redemption, it is termed corruptible. We tend to term things like fruit and vegetables as "corruptible" in that they have a short shelf life. Peter thinks of gold as corruptible although it has an almost unlimited "life." It therefore makes a fitting comparison to the enduring value of the precious blood of Christ.

The "way of life" we have been redeemed from is the pattern of life in which we lived without God. It was aimless, futile, and worthless. This is how Solomon described life without God. He used the corresponding word "vanity" thirteen times in the first two chapters of Ecclesiastes. Vanity is the sum total of the value of what we inherit from a culture where God is left out. In contrast, the Christian believer obtains "an inheritance incorruptible and undefiled and that does not fade away" (v. 4). We need to see that any culture without God is futile (Rom. 1:21).

We have been redeemed at infinite cost. The "blood of Christ" is a term that refers to Christ's death in all its saving aspects (compare Hebrews 9:14; 10:19; 1 John 1:7; Revelation 1:5). It is more precious because of its source, God's beloved Son. It is "precious" because of its comparison with the "aimless" way of life we are born into. Christ died to deliver us from this way of life. Christ's blood is described in terms of the lambs offered under the Old Testament sacrificial system. They were lambs "without blemish and without spot" (Num. 6:14). Jesus was the perfect "Lamb"; He was sinless, without any moral blemish. He was "the Lamb of God who takes away the sin of the world!" (John 1:29).

Christ Benefited Us with Redemption (1:20)

It was determined by agreement among the Godhead before the world was created that the Son would come to earth to pay a redemption price for His creatures (Rev. 13:8). In these "last times" Jesus was "manifest" (made known) by His suffering and resurrection. A similar passage in Hebrews says that, "God, who at various times and in various ways spoke in time past to the fathers by the prophets, has in these last days spoken to us by His Son" (Heb. 1:1-2). Other times when the Bible refers to "last times" it refers to the end times leading up to the second coming of Christ.

All this was "for your sake," that is, for the benefit of Peter's readers and, by application, to all believers in Christ. In verse 12 we learned that the prophecies about the Messiah in the Old Testament reveal how God has controlled salvation history. Now Peter summarizes the purpose for Christ's incarnation: to redeem a people for Himself. Knowing that the plan to redeem us has been in place since before the creation of the world, we should fear God and live holy lives.

Christ Is Glorified for Redeeming Us (1:21)

When the Son of God was made "manifest," He revealed God the Father (John 1:18). Jesus Himself said, "He who has seen Me has seen the Father" (John 14:9). It was through the manner of His life and His death that we have come to believe in God. The Father was satisfied with the Son's payment for sin and as a result raised Him from the dead and glorified Him (Rom. 1:4). The benefit for us is that our "faith and hope are in God" now—not in this world that offers no purpose for living or security for the future. We have much for which to thank and revere the Lord Jesus Christ!

Christians Are Obligated to Love One Another (1:22)

This third command, "love one another," complements the commands to be holy and to fear God in verses 13-21 but is reasoned on different grounds. Since Peter's readers were saved, it is most likely that the phrase "you have purified your souls in obeying the truth" refers to growth in moral purity. Other New Testament passages also use "purify" in reference to moral cleansing of believers progressing in holiness (James 4:8; 1 John 3:3). When we are "obeying the truth" we are responding in a practical way to all the truth of God's Word.

One way we show that we are obeying the Word is that we have a "sincere [genuine] love" for fellow believers. This love, empowered by the indwelling Holy Spirit, will flow from obedience to the truth. As Christian pilgrims, we will always be a minority in this world. We therefore need the close fellowship of our spiritual brothers and sisters, who may, like us, be suffering for believing in Christ. The love we demonstrate to one another should be an act of the will exercised for the good of others. Peter exhorts his readers to love "fervently," or intensely, and with a "pure heart," with integrity.

Source of the Power to Love One Another (1:23-25)

The basis for the exhortation to love one another springs from our having been born spiritually (v. 23). This life has been created by a spiritual seed. Peter describes the seed's character as "incorruptible" (compare vv. 18-19). In contrast to things in this passing world, the "seed," which is "the word of God," "lives and abides forever" (v. 23).

The incorruptible nature of "the word of God" is stressed in verse 24 by a reference from Isaiah 40:6-8. Human existence is fleeting and short-lived, like grass. The glory of man too is like the wildflowers in the field, which wither and die. These are contrasted with "the word of the LORD [which] endures forever." The term for "word" is not the usual one in the

New Testament, but a more specific one meaning "that which is spoken by the Lord." It is the message from God to men, specifically here the Christian gospel that had been "preached" (literally "evangelized") to Peter's readers in Asia Minor.

In this lesson on verses 13-25 about the pilgrim's holy behavior we have centered our thoughts on three specific commands given to first century pilgrim believers: "be holy," "conduct yourselves . . . in fear," and "love one another." All three commands are relevant to us today as well. Our character and conduct should match our calling.

CHAPTER

4

THE PILGRIM'S SPIRITUAL PRIESTHOOD (2:1-12)

Spiritual Growth Is Hindered by Sin (2:1)

Although there is a chapter break in our Bibles here, the first few verses in chapter 2 continue Peter's exhortation that he began at the end of chapter 1 (notice that verse 1 begins with the word "Therefore"). Verse 1 is also the first clause in a long sentence which runs through verse 3. In this verse, Peter emphasizes that loving one another "fervently with a pure heart" (1:22) demands that we get rid of every attitude and habit which may harm our brothers and sisters in Christ. The language is striking: "laying aside all malice, all deceit, hypocrisy, envy, and all evil speaking." Such attitudes have the effect of stunting our spiritual growth and causing us to have no desire for the Word of God.

Peter uses the imagery of taking off clothes. God's people are to get rid of the "old clothing" of our sinful nature as it does not reflect true Christian love. "Putting off the old" is a common New Testament metaphor (Eph. 4:22-25; Col. 3:8; Heb. 12:1; James 1:21). In this verse there are five items in the "old wardrobe" which must be put away. All of them aim at harming others; love, however, aims at helping others. As a minority group in the world, Christians should make every effort to treat one another well, not tear one another down.

The first sin Peter says to lay aside is malice, which is the attitude of ill will toward others, or wishing that bad things will happen to them. The second is deceit, which may take many forms in our dealings with others. The third is hypocrisy, which is a mask to cover inward evil by an outward show of righteousness, concealing our motives behind a pretense of holiness (Matt. 23:28; Mark 12:15). The fourth sin of the old nature to be discarded is envy. We are envious when we resent the successes or good fortune of others. Romans 12:15 says we should rejoice with those who rejoice. Finally, we should lay aside evil speaking of every kind. This reminds us of the ninth commandment: "You shall not bear false witness against your neighbor." Slander can be masked behind prayer requests or "I think you ought to know. . . ." All five of these are wicked sins of attitude and speech. They destroy, they do not build up. We as Christians are commanded to get rid of them.

Spiritual Growth Is Promoted by the Word of God (2:2-3)

The central idea here is that we should crave to grow spiritually. Just as infants have a longing for milk which they express loudly and frequently, so we are to have a craving for the Word of God because the Scriptures are our means of spiritual growth. The metaphor Peter used of babies craving for milk does not imply that his readers were baby Christians. Rather, it illustrates the *intensity* with which they should long for the Word continually.

The command is, "Desire the pure milk of the word, that you may grow thereby" (v. 2). "Pure milk" is a reference to the Word of God—our Bibles. In other passages, "milk" refers to the less complex truths of the Bible compared to the "solid food" of deeper truth (1 Cor. 3:2; Heb. 5:12-13). But here it refers to the Scriptures as spiritual growth food. Our aim should be to attain spiritual maturity. Only then can we become fully functional Christians.

Peter describes the Scriptures as "pure." Many false cults add what we might call "impurities" to the Scriptures—teachings that are not part of the canon of Scripture. He also describes them as "spiritual." This means that in contrast to literal milk, they are food for the soul and the spirit (1:23). We are *commanded* to crave the Word because the natural man does not. Even though we may not feel like it, we are to discipline ourselves to develop a taste and a craving for it. Spiritual growth from spiritual food is a command, not an option (2 Peter 3:18). The result is "that by it you may grow in respect to salvation." Salvation is our present possession as well as our future goal. It is sometimes termed *progressive sanctification,* and it requires our active cooperation with the Holy Spirit's work in us. Our lives are to be marked by continuous growth in the knowledge and likeness of God, nourished by the Word of God.

The command to crave the Word is based on the assumption that we have experienced the goodness of the Lord: "If indeed you have tasted that the Lord is gracious" (v. 3). These words remind us of the appeal in Psalm 34:8: "Oh, taste and see that the LORD is good." When we drink the milk of His Word we taste again and again what He is like. We first "tasted" His goodness when we believed on Christ as Savior. As we grow in respect to our salvation we gain an increasing thirst for more of His goodness and grace. What an encouragement to get into the Word! What a tragedy that the growth of so many Christians is stunted because they choose not to feed on it!

Christ Is the Living Stone (2:4)

As New Testament believers who have tasted God's grace expressed in salvation we have "come" to Christ, whom Peter describes in verse 4 as "a living stone." The word "stone" means a stone that is prepared and cut at the quarry to be placed in a building. Jesus called Himself "the stone" of Old Testament prophecy (Ps. 118:22; see also Matthew 21:42). He is a "living" Stone in contrast to inanimate stones that are used in constructing a building as well as being eternal with respect to His existence.

The living Stone was "rejected" by men (Luke 20:17-18) in contrast to having been accepted by those who "come" to Him. Peter implies that those who are "coming to Him" will experience opposition just as He did. Although men reject Christ and His followers, however, God has chosen Him and reckoned Him precious (v. 4). The same word "chosen" was applied to believers in 1:1. As the living Stone, Jesus Christ was specially chosen by God to be the indispensable Stone in the construction of His "house." Christ's value is priceless and He is destined for the place of highest honor in the "building."

The imagery of verse 4 pictures unbelieving men who have attempted to build a temple for God but who have rejected the most important "Stone" from the quarry, leaving it, as it were, lying unused in the weeds. Man-made religions have abounded throughout history, and many individuals try to come to God in their own way. But God has approved only one "way" by which we may be made acceptable to Him: through belief in His Son, the living Stone that men do not value.

Christians Are Living Stones (2:5a)

The subject turns from Christ the living Stone to believers who are living stones themselves being built into a spiritual house. The "house" is made up of all true believers and is the same as the true church (Eph. 2:19-20; Matt. 16:18). Believers are "living" stones because Christ has given us His life. We are "being built up [to] a spiritual house." The church will be complete when the Lord Jesus raptures it (1 Thess. 4:13-17).

The picture drawn here is from the Jewish temple which was the dwelling place of God on earth (1 Kings 6:12-13). The literal, physical temple had been made with stones; the new "people temple" is made of believers in Christ. They are indwelt by the Holy Spirit and the building they form is described as a "spiritual house." All believers are "being built together for a dwelling place of God in the Spirit" (Eph. 2:22). Peter wants us to appreciate the position we enjoy as stones in the spiritual temple where God dwells. The number of stones in this temple increases as people are saved. The quality of the temple improves as the "living" stones participate in their privileges.

Christians Are a Holy Priesthood (2:5b)

Peter goes on to describe a second function of believers in the new spiritual temple being built. Besides being living stones in the structure, we are also priests offering sacrifices. This passage teaches the wonderful truth that all believers are priests with direct access to God. This concept is one that relatively few of God's people understand fully. As we grasp this truth we can enter into our function as priests. The function of priesthood is not for a few specially chosen men as in Old Testament times; it is the privilege of *every* true believer in the Lord Jesus Christ. If you are a believer, you are already a priest with the privilege of offering spiritual sacrifices to God. There is no other priesthood for the church but the priesthood of all believers.

In the Old Testament the priests' role was to represent the Israelites to God. Only priests could present the offerings and sacrifices to God. Only priests could enter the holy sanctuary to offer incense and do other duties.

Only the high priest could enter the holiest place where the Ark of the Covenant stood, and then only once a year, on the Day of Atonement.

Since Christ's death, resurrection, and ascension, all that has changed. Immediately after Christ died, the veil of the temple was torn from top to bottom (Matt. 27:51). His great sacrifice is the basis on which our spiritual sacrifices are now acceptable to God (Heb. 10:12). He is now our Great High Priest through whom we, as priests, can "come boldly" (Heb. 4:14-16). We now have direct and equal access into God's presence, and He accepts our sacrifices "through Jesus Christ" (v. 5).

Our priesthood is described as "holy" because holiness reflects the character of God and the people of God (1:16). Like the priests in the Old Testament we are to offer sacrifices, but not animal sacrifices. Our sacrifices are spiritual in nature. They include praises to God (Heb. 13:15), sharing our possessions (Heb. 13:16), offering our bodies in service (Rom. 12:1-2), and giving money for the advance of the gospel (Phil. 4:18).

Christ Is the Chief Cornerstone (2:6)

Peter then supports the teaching of a "spiritual house" by stating that Christ is the cornerstone of this house, quoting from a prophecy in Isaiah 28:16. Isaiah prophesied that God would "lay in Zion a chief cornerstone, elect, precious" (v. 6). In verse 4, Peter mentioned that Christ was the "living stone, rejected indeed by men." Here in verse 6 he sees Christ as the "chief cornerstone," placed there by God. God has given the highest place of honor as cornerstone to the One whom men rejected.

Christ as the "chief cornerstone" is interpreted differently by Bible commentators, but we will mention just one interpretation here—that it was the initial stone in the corner of the building. As such it symbolizes the foundation on which the structure is built. First Corinthians 3:11 states that "No other foundation can anyone lay than that which is laid, which is Jesus Christ." Peter goes on to quote from the same prophecy in Isaiah 28:16: "And he who believes on Him will by no means be put to shame." The lesson we can draw is that no one who trusts in Him will ever be disappointed or have reason to regret putting their faith in Him. Christian pilgrims in this hostile world can trust Him. He is the solid foundation on which God has built His church, and He is a solid foundation on which to build one's own life (Matt. 7:24-25).

Christ Is the Stone of Stumbling (2:7-8)

In these two verses there is a sharp contrast between those who believe (Peter's readers) and those who do not. Addressing his believing readers, Peter says, "Therefore, to you who believe, He is precious" (v. 7). Because we are living stones in God's building, we highly value Him who is the Cornerstone. If He is not precious to us, something is wrong.

Peter goes on to quote two more Old Testament passages about those who disbelieve Christ, those who cast Him aside as worthless. He says, "The stone which the builders rejected has become the chief cornerstone" (Ps. 118:22). This word "cornerstone" is not the same Greek word Peter used for "cornerstone" in verse 6. Literally it is the "head or top of the corner," like the capstone of a pyramid. The capstone is the unique stone in the structure and occupies the highest place, taking the shape and angles of the structure as a whole. God has given Christ the highest place of honor, but the men who reject Him "stumble" over Him.

Peter quotes from Isaiah 8:14, revealing that the "Capstone" they reject causes them to stumble and fall (v. 8). Observe carefully the reason why they stumble: "They stumble, being disobedient to the word." The unbelieving world in Peter's day, as in ours, had willfully disobeyed and rejected the moral standards revealed in Scripture. They were offended by the holy Son of God, preferring their sinful ways to the salvation from sin He offered (John 3:19). They rejected God's way of salvation (John 5:40).

The section closes with a phrase that has troubled some Bible students: "They stumble . . . to which they also were appointed." This does not mean that God destines some to disobey the Word and be lost eternally. It teaches that the rejecters, those who consciously and deliberately disobey God's Word, are destined to stumble—this will be the outcome of their choice of rejecting the Son. In the whole passage the emphasis is placed on their disobedience and not on God's making a choice. God does not choose that *any* people should perish. However, Peter's concern is to comfort these pilgrim believers under persecution. Eventually, those who reject Christ will "fall" in the sense that they will be judged eternally for rejecting Christ.

Christians Are a Royal Priesthood (2:9-10)

In contrast to those who reject and therefore stumble over Christ, Peter points to those who accept Christ and acknowledge Him as the precious, chosen Cornerstone. The contrast is drawn by the words "But you." They are called a "chosen generation, a royal priesthood, a holy nation, His own special people." These four privileges for believers are added to those we have already noted in verse 5. The very same privileges were offered to Israel when the Law was given at Mount Sinai if they would obey God (Exod. 19:5-6). But the Israelites did not obey and therefore lost the privileges. God now gives them to those who are "coming to Him as to a living stone" (v. 4).

True believers are a "chosen generation" from before the creation of the world (Eph. 1:4). We are not chosen as a physical family like the Jews were, who had Abraham as their ancestor. We are a spiritual family, born of God and indwelt by the Spirit of God. Believers also form a "holy nation." Israel had been set apart by God to be marked by holiness as nation. Because Israel failed, the nation has been set aside until a future time. Meanwhile the true church is God's "holy nation." The fourth description of believers is "His own special people." This emphasizes God's ownership. God had called Israel "My people" (Deut. 7:6; Isa. 43:21). They have temporarily lost that distinction (Hos. 1:9), but it will be restored to them in the millennium and experienced on the earth (Hos. 2:23; Zech. 8:8). Meanwhile the church is God's special possession, His "people" for this age, because God's purposes on earth are being carried out through her. The church will ultimately be Christ's heavenly people.

All four of these privileges are given to us as a "royal priesthood" that we may "proclaim the praises of Him who called [us] out of darkness into His marvelous light" (v. 9) This refers to God's evangelistic purpose for the church. We are to "proclaim"—literally, to make widely known—the excellencies of God, not our own experiences. We are never to lose the wonder of the truth that He has "called us" out of spiritual darkness into His wonderful light. Now "in the light," we declare God's preeminence in all that He is and does.

In verse 10 the transformation from darkness to light is further explained with two "before and after" contrasts. They apply to Peter's initial readers and to us too. "Who once were not a people, but are now the people of God." In our pre-Christian lives they served no useful purpose in God's program. They were "no people," but now they are God's special people for His great purposes. The verse contains another contrast, "Who had not obtained mercy but now have obtained mercy." These contrasting statements should help us appreciate all that God has saved us *from* and what He has saved us *for.*

Christians Are to Be a Pure Testimony (2:11-12)

This section is a strong appeal ("I beg you") to those whom Peter has been addressing as a "holy priesthood" and a "royal priesthood" to *live* like priests of the God they represent as a testimony to the pagan world around them. He calls them "Beloved" to assure them of his loving concern for their spiritual lives.

Note that the theme of their pilgrim life continues—Peter describes them "as sojourners and pilgrims" in the world, with no status and no rights. The pilgrimage theme has appeared three times so far (1:1, 17; 2:11). In light of this, they are to "abstain from fleshly lusts which war against the soul." In chapter 1:14, Peter told them not to let their lives be molded by these "desires." Here he tells them to avoid worldly desires completely. As pilgrims in the world we are like fish swimming through many attractive lures in which lie deadly hooks. We are to deliberately avoid them because they are really weapons designed to attack our spiritual lives.

Instead of giving in to worldly desires, we are to live such good lives that they powerfully convict the world of its own sin. The world, then as now, built a case against Christians and slandered them publicly. The "day of visitation" in verse 12 is without an article and may be defined as "a day when God visits," either to bring blessing or judgment. If it means it will bring judgment, then it refers to the future day of judgment when the "Gentiles" will be forced to admit that they were wrong and everything these Christians were saying was right (Phil: 2:10-11). They will glorify God just as Joshua said Aachan would by publicly confessing his sin (Josh. 7:19). God receives glory when His name and His righteous standards are vindicated.

If the phrase means that God's visitation will bring blessing, we understand it to mean that those pagan people who were currently slandering Christians would be saved by observing their good works and responding by putting their faith in Christ. Thus, even those pagans will one day glorify God. In the next chapter Peter gives an example of this when he says that husbands may be converted when they see the godly behavior of their Christian wives (3:1-2).

5

THE PILGRIM'S PRACTICAL SUBMISSION (2:13–3:7)

Christians are meant to live in the public arena where their behavior can be a testimony to people in a watching—albeit hostile—world. Peter now focuses on one very visible aspect of behavior: submission to authority. We abuse freedom as believers if we assume that our citizenship in heaven puts us above earthly authority structures. While we are pilgrims on earth we are subject to those whom God has placed over us here. Ultimately all Christian obedience is to God, but it is usually exercised in the context of human institutions like the three that are in focus in this passage: civil government, the workplace, and marriage. God established these so that human life and society can function in an orderly way.

The Principle of Submission (2:13)

Peter begins with a general statement. "Therefore submit yourselves to every ordinance of man for the Lord's sake." The phrase "every ordinance" refers to boundaries that have been set by human institutions. Peter takes three areas of authority in turn and explains how believers should submit to them. The principle of submission also applies to other authority structures, such as children to parents and members of the local church to their elders. The general rule is, "submit . . . for the Lord's sake." The *exception* to the rule is that believers should resist a command to sin. For biblical examples of this scenario, see Daniel 3:13-18; Daniel 6:10-24; Acts 4:18-20; and Acts 5:27-29.

Submit to Civil Government (2:13-17)

Civil government is the first example given (vv. 13-17). In speaking of civil authorities, the apostle Paul said in Romans 13:1 that "the authorities that exist are appointed by God." Submit to kings—even to evil kings such as Nero, who was emperor of Rome when Peter wrote this letter. Believers should submit to civil law, which includes paying taxes and obtaining licenses, because God ordained civil authority.

The Government's Responsibilities (vv. 13-14)

The purpose for which God ordained civil government is stated in verse 14: "for the punishment of evildoers and for the praise of those who do good." Governments have the right to punish offenders appropriately for the evil committed. Note that punishment is the duty of governments, not of the individual who may have been wronged (Rom. 12:17-21). And in the same way that punishment is a deterrent to evil, so praise and reward are encouragements to do right. Governments are to honor moral integrity. Christians should therefore pray for good government (1 Tim. 2:1-4).

The Christian's Responsibilities (vv. 15-17)

Peter now explains why Christians should submit to government. First, God has designed Christian behavior to affect secular government. "For this is the will of God, that by doing good you may put to silence the ignorance of foolish men" (v. 15). When believers obey civil rulers they put an end to irrational slander and false accusations. Upright and law-abiding Christian behavior will ultimately silence their foolishness.

Obedience to a godless government might have seemed very restrictive to a Christian who understood his pilgrim status, so Peter says that "doing good" by obeying the government is not restrictive. It is true freedom when we are free from the bondage of believing that government must serve our personal comforts. When we obey a harsh ruler, we are "doing good" by choice and are therefore free.

In this passage, by doing good the Christian uses his freedom to choose a lifestyle that pleases God. This is not always easy to do when the authorities are blatantly corrupt. Christian freedom, however, is balanced by Christian responsibility. It operates only in the realm of righteousness. Real freedom comes only in complete submission to God, when we view ourselves as His bondservants (v. 16). We now see ourselves as free to do what is *right,* not what is wrong.

Note four responsibilities in verse 17 for those who freely choose to obey God. "Honor all people" refers to the respect and courtesy due to all human beings. The word "people" is not in the original Greek text, so the emphasis is on the word "all." Peter then reminds the believers once again to "love the brotherhood" of true Christians as the family of God (1:22) and to "fear God"—hold God in reverential awe—which leads to obedience. Finally, they should "honor the king," the ruler of the land, because God has placed him in authority over them. The word "honor" is the same word as in the first command to "honor all people."

Submit in the Workplace (2:18-25)

In this section, Peter speaks to "servants" using a word that refers to household servants. These were not only domestic staff; many were skilled in trades and professions. They were owned as slaves but were often well paid and enjoyed privileges. They represented the most common workers in the Roman world. Today, those of us who are more or less bound to our jobs in the workplace can appropriately apply the principles taught here.

Submit to All Kinds of Employers (v. 18)

Harsh employers were a fact of life in the Roman Empire, just as now. Peter speaks to believers who work for them. "Be submissive to your masters with all fear, not only to the good and gentle, but also to the harsh." Christian employees should willingly obey their bosses with "all fear." We fear employers when we respect their authority and respond to their demands. We should not disdain or carelessly disregard their orders, even when the demands are "harsh." This word in the original Greek means "crooked." Laban was a "crooked" employer; he treated his son-in-law Jacob harshly, expecting a lot from him under difficult working conditions. He changed Jacob's wages ten times, but God took care of Jacob (Gen. 31:6-9). We are to submit to our employers for the Lord's sake unless commanded to sin, in which case we are to say no.

Submit to Employers Because God Is Sovereign (vv. 19-20)

We should submit to "crooked" employers because "this is commendable," which means that God approves such submission. God's approval should govern our responses to the boss at work. We obey because of "conscience toward God," which means that we obey because we sense the reality of God's sovereignty over our circumstances. Knowing that

God is there and that He is in control gives us the key to enduring a harsh boss who may treat us badly. We will then escape the trap of self-pity and resentment that mistreatment often tempts us to fall prey to. Of course, one option usually open to employees today which may not have been so in Peter's day is the ability to resign and work elsewhere.

The "grief" and "suffering" (v. 20) refer to the various kinds of mental anguish that go along with unreasonable demands made by an employer. If we suffer because we have done wrong we do not, of course, deserve any special commendation—we deserve rebuke instead. It is when we suffer for doing right and patiently endure the consequences that we have the commendation of God.

Follow Christ's Example in Submitting to Suffering (2:21-25)

Patiently enduring suffering for doing right is pleasing to God. Peter now sets before us the example of how the Lord Jesus Christ dealt with unjust treatment. "Christ also suffered . . . leaving us an example, that you should follow His steps" (v. 21). Peter gives us the most compelling example, because in the wisdom of God we are all "called" to endure suffering. When we are saved, God summons us to a life which may include suffering unjustly. If that suffering comes, remember two things: (1) God uses it for your good with the future in view (Rom. 5:1-3; 1 Peter 4:13). (2) The Lord Jesus is your example. He also suffered.

The word "example" was used in New Testament times of a drawing by a master artist that he would place before his students for them to imitate. Thus, when we are mistreated, we are to imitate Jesus' response when He was mistreated. He responded by trusting in God's plan rather than attacking His attackers. The key to enduring, which we learn from the Lord Jesus, is yielding to God. Peter calls us to "follow His steps." Christ's faith in the good purposes of the Father allowed Him to endure it. The issue of "following" was a familiar one to Peter. When Jesus called him to be His disciple He had said to him, "Follow me" (Mark 1:16-17). And His last words to Peter were, "Follow me" (John 21:19-22).

Christ Did Not Sin (v. 22)

Note several other things about the example Christ left for us to follow. First, He suffered without sinning. "'Who committed no sin, nor was deceit found in His mouth'." Peter borrowed this language from Isaiah's great prophecy of the suffering Servant written seven hundred years earlier (Isa. 53:9). Note particularly the emphasis that there was never any pretense or deceitfulness in His speech. The tongue is often the first human faculty to fail under pressure, but the Lord never sinned with His tongue. Christian employees in today's world have the same temptations to sin with their tongues in the workplace. They too must follow the example of the One who always spoke with integrity.

Christ Did Not Retaliate (v. 23)

The Lord Jesus never retaliated against those who mistreated Him. "When He was reviled, did not revile in return; when He suffered, He did not threaten, but committed Himself to Him who judges righteously." Christ never even uttered a harsh word during the trials before Caiaphas and Pilate when He was being intensely provoked by insults. Peter had retaliated with a sword against those who came to arrest Jesus, but Jesus rebuked him, saying, "Shall I not drink the cup which My Father has given Me?" (John 18:11). He could endure because He had accepted that the "cup" of suffering was necessary to accomplish the plan of salvation.

Christ Suffered in His Body (v. 24a)

A third aspect to Christ being an example of unjust suffering is that He endured it in His human body. "Who Himself bore our sins *in His own body* on the tree" (v. 24, emphasis added). The human body is the vehicle in which we endure suffering of all kinds—physical, mental, and emotional—but the suffering is temporary. Christ's sufferings were, of course unique. When He was crucified He was cruelly treated by man and also bore God's wrath against sin. It's a comfort to know that because our bodies only relate to life on this earth, whatever suffering we go through is related to this earth and is therefore temporary, just as Christ's was.

Christ Suffered for a Reason (v. 24b)

Suffering within the will of God is not an end in itself. Peter goes on to illustrate from Christ's sufferings that there is purpose behind it. The purpose of Christ's suffering was: "that we, having died to sins, might live for righteousness." The phrase "having died to sins" is an important doctrine. Jesus did not only die *in our place;* we also died *with Him* in the sense that we identify with God's condemnation of sin. (Hanging on a tree was a means of death that God had cursed. See Galatians 3:13.) In effect, we agree with God about sin and we now count our old sinful life as dead. Paul put it this way: "knowing this, that our old man was crucified with Him . . . that we should no longer be slaves of sin" (Rom. 6:6)

We now notice the positive side of this truth, which is Peter's main emphasis here: "that we . . . might live for righteousness." Having agreed with God's condemnation of sin, we are to make progress in righteous living. Paul said in Romans 6:13: "And do not present your members as instruments of unrighteousness to sin, but present yourselves to God as being alive from the dead and your members as instruments of righteousness to God." Christ suffered with this purpose in mind.

A related effect of Christ's suffering is that we are "healed" by Christ's "stripes"—another quote from Isaiah 53. Stripes refer to the welts left by scourging, which was a common form of punishment in Roman times. Any mistreated slaves to whom Peter was writing would identify easily with the very mention of it. Jesus endured the stroke of divine judgment at Calvary, which resulted in our wholeness and spiritual healing. (The context clearly indicates that the "healing" is spiritual and was accomplished at the cross. It does not refer to physical healing today.)

Christ Reconciled Us to God (v. 25)

As a result of being healed and made whole, our relationship with God has been restored. "For you were like sheep going astray, but have now returned to the Shepherd and Overseer of your souls." Our former lost condition is pictured as sheep straying from the shepherd. Once again Peter refers to Isaiah 53 (v. 6). But, he says, you have now returned (or turned about) to the Shepherd. Read Mark 14:27, John 10:1-18, Hebrews 13:20, and 1 Peter 5:4 for other New Testament references to Christ as a Shepherd. As our Shepherd He leads, provides, feeds, and protects His sheep. He is also the Overseer, or Guardian, in that He has taken care of the well-being of our souls in reconciling us to God.

As a witness to Christ's sufferings, Peter could look back and see what it had accomplished. In exhorting us to follow Christ's steps, we can be encouraged that any suffering we endure unjustly has some good purpose for our spiritual welfare (Rom. 8:28).

Submit in the Home (3:1-7)

The third area where submission is to be practiced is in the home. Peter now speaks to wives and husbands. In the Christian's submissive role in government and work place, Peter only spoke to the person under authority. In his discussion of the home, he speaks to both roles in the marriage relationship. Peter's aim was to give the Christian wife a strategy for disarming the hostility of her unbelieving husband and so win him for Christ by her submission. He then concludes with advice for Christian husbands.

Wives, Submit to Husbands (vv. 1-2)

The section begins by linking the wife's role to the phrase in 2:18, "Servants, be submissive." The text reads, "Wives, likewise, be submissive." Peter does not imply that wives are the same as servants. The word "likewise" does not mean "exactly like," but a softer term meaning "in a similar way." The similarity is in the motive—both servants and wives should submit "for the Lord's sake" (2:13). The wife, like the servant, should take the initiative to submit to their God-given authority figure. Whenever submission is exhorted in Scripture, it is never meant to be enforced by another (e.g. Eph. 5:21-22). In other words, the husband should not make his wife place herself under his authority.

The wife's attitude is also to be similar to that of servants in her attempt to please her husband. She should not want to incur His displeasure even when he is far from perfect. Her submission is a key to the biblical marriage relationship. Like the roles of citizens and servants already discussed, the wife's role is never reversed in Scripture. Husbands are never told to be subject to their wives. However, we should remember that the role of submission does not imply inferiority as a person. Husband and wife are equal as people, but there is a distinction in the roles they take in marriage. This is God's ordained order. Thus the final responsibility for decisions affecting the family will be the husband's. God's order is beautiful when it is motivated by love.

The purpose for the wife's submission is for her husband's spiritual blessing—that some, though they "do not obey the word . . . may be won by the conduct of their wives." Unbelieving husbands may well have a lifestyle characterized by disobedience to God's moral standards as well as to His invitation to salvation. But this is just the situation in which the

Christian wife's behavior may win him. In fact, often the less she pleads with him to be saved and the more she demonstrates salvation by her godly submission, the greater the impact on her husband for God. Her husband will observe her "chaste conduct accompanied by fear." Even though he is hostile to her faith he will respect her moral purity in a corrupt world. He also notices her fear and reverence for God. He can't miss her purity and her piety. In relation to him she remains a helper suitable for him. That has been God's order since creation.

Wives, Have a Gentle Spirit (vv. 3-4)

The apostle Peter now goes a step further in instructing how wives should win their husbands to Christ: not with external beauty, but with true inner beauty. Some Christians have used verse 3 to forbid the use of any jewelry or new style of clothing, but that misses the point. This passage is saying that these are not the things that will lead to a husband's salvation. Her source of beauty is not primarily external but "the hidden person of the heart"—her inner character. Though not as obvious as clothing and ornaments, it is revealed indirectly through her words and attitude. Her beautiful character outshines her outward appearance. She possesses the "incorruptible beauty of a gentle and quiet spirit." The word "incorruptible" is used in the New Testament of things that are heavenly and which will not pass away. Here is the true beauty of godly womanhood.

Gentleness is a characteristic of the nine-fold fruit of the Spirit (Gal. 5:22-23). It is often translated as "meekness" and is the opposite of being pushy and demanding. It is seen most perfectly in the Lord Jesus Christ who said, "I am gentle and lowly in heart" (Matt. 11:29). Even unbelieving husbands may be attracted by this kind of beauty, which is more than "skin deep." It is also "very precious in the sight of God." God delights in gentleness because it comes from deep confidence and trust in Him.

Wives, Follow Sarah's Example (vv. 5-6)

Peter illustrates the principle of submission in marriage by reminding his readers of "holy women who trusted in God" (v. 5). They too adorned themselves with a gentle and quiet spirit—it was their style of life. Here too, as in verse 3, their submissive behavior is described as an "ornament" of inward beauty. It is their confidence in God which enabled them to submit to their husbands' authority with the assurance that their ultimate good was being served.

Sarah is the specific example of a submissive wife: "as Sarah obeyed Abraham, calling him lord" (v. 6). This is probably not a reference to any specific incident, but rather to the long term pattern of her life with Abraham. For her, to follow Abraham meant trusting God, and sometimes in difficult and even dangerous circumstances (Gen. 12:1, 5, 10-15; 13:1; 20:2-6; 22:3).

Godly wives are described as Sarah's "daughters" (v. 6). This means that, like Sarah, they are the heirs of God's promise. Notice that the promise is conditional: "If you do good and are not afraid with any terror." We are to follow Sarah in her doing "good," but not in her wrongdoing (Gen. 16:2-6; 18:15). And like Sarah, we are not to fear, but trust God.

Husbands, Honor Your Wives (v. 7)

The section on submission in the home closes with two significant commands for Christian husbands on how to use their God-given authority over their wives. First, they should "dwell with them with understanding." They should know the needs, desires, and even the frustrations of their wives. True understanding will lead to his sympathetic response to her. The wife is the "weaker" vessel, but note that this implies that the husband is "weak" also. Wives are weaker not only because of their physical strength, but also because of their marital vows of submission. Her husband must not take advantage of her role.

The second duty of the husband is to give "honor to the wife." He is to treat her as a highly valuable ornamental bowl or vessel, protecting her beauty and praising her qualities. He should give priority to her choices and affirm her ideas and actions. Peter points out that she complements him as being fellow "heirs together of the grace of life." This may refer to life on earth, but more probably refers to their eternal inheritance. It is necessary so that the husbands' prayers will not be "hindered." Note that domestic failure will result in their spiritual loss. Thus the duties of husbands are vital both to their marital happiness and their spiritual well-being.

6

The Pilgrim's Suffering for Righteousness (3:8-22)

Peter has been urging us, as temporary residents in this world and pilgrims on our way to heaven, to maintain excellent behavior among non-believers. Our conduct is a powerful witness to them (2:12; 3:1). Part of that witness is to submit to authority structures in the nation, in the workplace, and in the home. In this section he gives further instruction to "all" of us (v. 8) as to our public testimony.

Behavior Among Believers (3:8)

Godly responses begin with godly attitudes. Peter stresses five attitudes that are very similar in nature which will help us live in peace with our fellow Christians. "Finally all of you be of one mind, having compassion for one another, love as brothers, be tender hearted, be courteous." To be of the same mind does not mean that Christians must all have the same opinion about every issue, but that we share the common purpose of glorifying God. With that purpose before us, differences will blend in harmony rather than clash in discord. Jesus prayed for this kind of unity when He prayed that "they may be one" (John 17:21).

"Having compassion for one another" is to be sympathetic to the needs of others, to enter into their feelings. It is weeping with those who weep (Rom. 12:15). "Love as brothers" refers to mutual love for one another in the family of God as His children; this is the third time Peter has made this exhortation (1:22; 2:17). We are to demonstrate our family bonds by support, encouragement, and help. To be tender hearted is to be deeply sensitive to the needs of others. A related expression is often used of the Lord Jesus Christ: "He was moved with compassion" (Matt. 9:36).

The fifth attitude is courtesy—a quality very lacking today. It involves treating people with respect and echoes a similar appeal in 2:17. Active courtesy is more than expressing social etiquette; it is thoughtfulness and consideration for others. When believers treat one another this way, it glorifies God and is a testimony to the world by showing that our belonging to Christ does make a radical difference in attitudes and actions (John 13:35).

Behavior to Unbelievers (3:9)

Unbelievers were insulting these first century Christians and speaking evil of them. Paul spoke of the way the apostles were being treated when he said, "We have been made as the filth of the world." The way they responded, however, was, "being reviled, we bless; being persecuted, we endure" (1 Cor. 4:12-13). The natural human impulse is to retaliate against such treatment; the biblical response is to reject that impulse, "not returning evil for evil, or reviling for reviling, but on the contrary blessing" (v. 9). Instead of snapping back with a sarcastic insult, we treat them with kindness (Rom. 12:17-21). Jesus told His disciples to "bless those who curse you" (Luke 6:28). It is not an easy assignment. Often the best way to bless them is to pray for them.

We should understand that opposition and hostility can come and therefore not be caught off guard when they do. More than that, in God's perfect plan, we are "called to this"—to return blessing for evil (v. 9), just as we are called to be patient in suffering (2:20-21). The result of blessing those who insult us is that we "inherit a blessing." The "blessing" we inherit is a different word from the "blessing" we give. What we inherit is the favorable regard God gives in this life to those who bless when insulted. He gives His special protection and care to His people who are suffering. Peter had already referred to some of the spiritual blessings we have in this life, like assurance of salvation, joy, redemption, priesthood, mercy, God's shepherding care, conversion of unbelieving husbands, and answered prayer for considerate husbands. That the blessings Peter is thinking of here are also related to this life and not to our future life in heaven is made clear by the supporting quote in verses 10 through 12 from Psalm 34.

David's Formula for "The Good Life" (3:10-12)

Verse 9 is Peter's commentary on Psalm 34:12-16. Note several things that Peter wants to bring to the attention of his readers from the psalm. First, there is the Christian zest for living—to "love life and see good days." Life is worth living in spite of persecution when we know that God is in control and that "all things work together for good to them who love God" (Rom. 8:28). We should even view the difficult days as "good" days because we "have eyes" to see God's glory displayed in meaningful ways.

Second, to see good days requires we discipline ourselves not to do evil. "Let him refrain his tongue from evil and his lips from seeking deceit" (v. 10). That is, we must hold back from saying anything that does not glorify God. It is putting aside "all guile," or pretense, saying one thing and meaning another (compare 2:1 and 2:21-23). We must take appropriate action to achieve this, that is, take evasive action to avoid it (v. 11). We are to have a holy aversion to this sin.

Third, we can see good days by doing good and seeking peace (v. 11). It is often very difficult to have peaceful relations with those who are against us. We must therefore aggressively pursue peace, taking initiative where we can. Retaliation will only intensify any attack, but meekness with patient endurance will defuse it and promote peace (Prov. 15:1).

The fourth ingredient in the "formula" for enjoying good days is to rest in God's promise of His gracious concern for persecuted pilgrims. Still quoting from Psalm 34, Peter says, "For the eyes of the Lord are on the righteous, and His ears are open to their prayers." We are never out of God's sight and never out of His earshot. He hears our faintest cry. What comfort this brings to stressed believers! But notice that the promise for answered prayer is only for "the righteous." There is a close connection between the practical righteousness of our lives and having our prayers answered. The final phrase of the quote from Psalm 34 says, "But the face of the Lord is against those who do evil." The persecutors were primarily in view. God's "face" indicates His personal presence, whether for blessing or in judgment. In this case it is for judgment against evildoers. This reminder should encourage all Christians who are undergoing persecution—God, the just Judge, will avenge His suffering children in His time (Rom. 12:17-21).

How to Cope with Persecution (3:13-17)

The subject moves to some very practical instructions on how to think and act when persecution does come. Peter starts with a rhetorical question which makes the point that those who are zealous for the good are not usually persecuted. "And who is he who will harm you if you become followers of what is good?" (v. 13) Most English versions use a much stronger word than "followers" in our NKJV text. "Eager" or "zealous" for good is closer to the idea. When we energetically work for the welfare of others, we are much less likely to suffer from our fellow men. So the first thing is to remember is that suffering is not the normal expectation for law-abiding, hard-working, peace-seeking believers.

The Blessing of Suffering for Christ (v. 14)

Peter goes on to say, however, that when suffering does come, it is a blessing. "But even if you should suffer for righteousness' sake, you are blessed." Peter echoes the words of the Lord Jesus here. Early in His teaching, in the Sermon on the Mount, the Lord Jesus explained to His disciples that the hurt of suffering is for His sake (Matt. 5:11). Suffering for "righteousness" sake is a direct result of doing good. Peter's point is that when this kind of persecution happens to you, you are blessed, and your suffering is not wasted. The blessing is God's favorable regard toward you when you honor Him through the trial. With this perspective, you "count it all joy," as James says (James 1:2). To be "blessed" is to enjoy God's special regard for them because they are suffering for Christ's sake.

The knowledge of God's favor means that we do not need to fear threats, nor be troubled. The Old Testament quote in verse 14 is taken from the prophet Isaiah's writings. He told King Ahaz of Judah not to be fearful (literally, "shaken up") when the enemy conspired against the nation as God was faithfully working out His purposes and was with them (Isa. 8:10-22). *We* should not be shaken by intimidation, either. Jesus used the same word when He encouraged His disciples in the Upper Room just before His crucifixion: "Let not your hearts be troubled" (John 14:27).

Sanctify Christ as Lord (v. 15)

Verse 15 tells us how to deal with the fear which comes when we are threatened and intimidated for doing good. "But sanctify Christ as Lord in your hearts." These words are Peter's paraphrase of part of the Isaiah passage referred to in verse 14. Isaiah said, "Do not . . . be afraid of their threats nor be troubled. The Lord of Hosts, Him shall you hallow" (Isa. 8:12-13). Notice carefully that Peter, by inspiration of the Holy Spirit, replaced Isaiah's command to sanctify (hallow) the Lord of Hosts with saying we are to sanctify *Christ* as Lord. This is a text that supports Jesus Christ's deity.

To sanctify Christ as Lord in our hearts is to treat Him as holy and sacred in the core of our being. It is to acknowledge Christ as being in control of our lives and our circumstances. When we set Him apart as sovereign in our hearts, we need not live in fear of circumstances. In a positive sense, we consciously yield to Him. Everything we think and say and do is to be deliberately placed under His control. Of course, to enthrone the Lord Jesus Christ in our hearts means that self must be taken off the throne.

With Christ as Lord in our hearts we must be ready to defend the hope we have as Christians. Because the world system hates the Lord Jesus, it also hates His followers and opposes what we stand for (John 15:18-19). We must be ready to give a rational account of our "hope" when challenged. It is, after all, a "living hope" (1:3). We answer with the truth and seize the opportunity to witness for Christ.

To answer our critics and at the same time testify of the hope within us involves having the right attitudes. The text says, "With meekness and godly fear" (v. 15c). Meekness will make us gentle and polite, which is difficult when hostile people are hurling accusations. Winning people is more important than winning arguments. Having a healthy fear of bringing the truth of God into disrepute will keep us from being arrogant or argumentative. It will help us depend on God for strength to please Him.

Keep a Good Conscience (vv. 16-17)

Meekness toward our opponents and fear toward God are to be accompanied by "a good conscience." Conscience is the ability to evaluate the right or wrong of something and to act accordingly. Our opponents may seek to defame us and slander our good conduct, but a good conscience will allow us to not be adversely affected by their slander. The more we are like Christ—gentle, truthful, fearing God—the more annoyed our opponents may become, because our conduct puts them to shame. But the Christ-like believer can act with poise because his conscience is clear.

Peter adds a related principle in verse 17: "For it is better, if it is the will of God, to suffer for doing good than for doing evil." Suffering for doing good is one thing; we can be assured that it is often within God's will for us for our spiritual blessing and maturity. But there is no profit or value in any suffering we may endure for doing wrong.

Christ Is Our Example of Suffering and Exaltation (3:18-22)

The final paragraph in chapter 3 brings encouragement to suffering Christians. "For Christ also suffered once for sins, the just for the unjust, that He might bring us to God." In this remarkable statement, Peter wants his readers to be aware of several things. One is that they themselves were "brought to God" via Christ's suffering, so it should not surprise them when their own efforts to bring others to God result in their own suffering. Peter also wants to encourage them by pointing out that Christ's suffering ended in the triumph of resurrection, ascension, and dominion (vv. 18, 22). Thus they too can look beyond their time of hardship to a future and complete salvation when they themselves will be victors with their Lord. This is the theme of the whole section and echoes what Peter wrote in 2:19-24.

Christ's Suffering on the Cross (v. 18)

Peter begins with a wonderful summary statement of the meaning of Christ's suffering on the cross which goes far beyond his purpose of encouraging the suffering saints. Christ's sufferings at Calvary were unique. Four aspects of it are evident here.

1. He suffered "for sins." That is, He bore the penalty for the sin of mankind on the cross, probably during the three hours of darkness (Matt. 27:46-47).

2. He suffered "once," putting an end to the daily and annual sacrifices of the Jews which did not take away sins anyway (Heb. 10:10-14).

3. He suffered as "the just for the unjust," meaning that His sinless character qualified Him to bear the sins of sinners.

4. He suffered "that He might bring us to God." Our sins once separated us from God, but Christ's death bridged the gap and reconciled us to Him.

Verse 18 concludes with a contrast between Christ's death and His resurrection life. Translators are divided over the phrase in our text, "made alive by the Spirit." The New American Standard Version favors the translation "made alive in the spirit," which more clearly indicates the contrast of parallel phrases "put to death in the flesh, but made alive in the spirit." Christ's physical death as a flesh-and-blood man on earth is contrasted with His risen life as the glorified Lord. "Flesh" and "spirit" indicate the two spheres of His existence as the incarnate Son of God. He was on earth "in the flesh" and He subsequently rose to a new sphere "in the spirit." His crucifixion was a violent and bodily death in the human sphere of His existence. In contrast, His resurrection lifted Him out of the earthly sphere and into the heavenly. Peter's suffering readers would be encouraged that they too could look forward to being lifted out of the earthly sphere in which they were suffering and into the spiritual, heavenly sphere.

Christ's Extensive Victory after the Cross (vv. 19-21)

Verse 19 is one of the most intriguing and puzzling in the New Testament: "By whom also He went and preached to the spirits in prison." Who are the spirits in prison? When did Christ preach to them? And what did He preach? There are five major views on these questions held by sincere scholars. For this study we will simply explain the view which we believe best fits the passage and the context. Interested students will want to do further study on their own.

The first phrase is best rendered "in which," because it refers to the spiritual realm into which Christ was raised from the dead (see comments above on verse 18). The term "spirits" is consistently applied to supernatural beings in the Bible. Here it refers to beings known to us as fallen angels (see Jude 6 and 2 Peter 2:4). We believe they are the "sons of God" referred to in Genesis 6:1-8 and Job 1:6. (The term "sons of God" is used in Scripture only of those directly created by God and can apply to angels and Adam in the old creation and to believers in the new creation.) In Genesis 6:1-8 the biblical record speaks of the sons of God cohabiting with the "daughters of men" and producing a corrupt race of giants called "nephilim." The resulting violence, wickedness, and perversion of morality caused God to say, "I will destroy man whom I have created from the face of the earth" (Gen. 6:7).

When Christ rose from the dead, He ascended through the realm of the "prince of the power of the air, the spirit who now works in the sons of disobedience" (Eph. 2:2). When He ascended, He "disarmed principalities and powers . . . made a public spectacle of them, triumphing over them in it" (Col. 2:15). He then took His seat at the right hand of the Father "far above all principality and power and might and dominion . . . and put all things under His feet" (Eph. 1:21-22).

To these spirits "in prison" Christ went and preached. Where He went is not clearly stated, but the language implies a definite place. It may be somewhere in the heavens where Satan and his angels are until the time when they will be cast out (Rev. 12:7-9). What Christ preached or proclaimed to them was the announcement of His triumph accomplished over sin and death at the cross and in His resurrection. Satan and his hosts were defeated, and the victorious Christ made a public display of them (Col. 2:15).

The disobedience of the wicked spirits took place "formerly" (v. 20), that is, during Noah's lifetime, before the flood. Genesis 6 and 2 Peter 2:4-5 also connect the disobedience of the angel-spirits and the days of Noah. God did not immediately respond in judgment on them when they sinned. Our verse tells us that the "divine longsuffering waited" during the time it took Noah to build the ark (120 years). God is never eager to pour out His wrath. He waited as the perverted wickedness grew worse and worse.

Peter encouraged the persecuted believers with the example of Christ who had first endured the hostility of sinners and then triumphed, going to the extent of proclaiming victory to the condemned, wicked spirits of long ago. These believers, too, could look beyond their present circumstances to ultimate victory in Christ. Not only would they be encouraged that the future was bright for them, but also that it would bring judgment for God's enemies.

Now Peter further encourages them by citing the example of the "eight souls [who] were saved through water," the believers who lived in the wicked world before the flood. They also triumphed in that God delivered them from the judgment which destroyed the world. "This also is an antitype which now saves us—namely baptism" (v. 21). Christian baptism is described as an antitype, or counterpart of the type, just as a stamped address on the envelope is the counterpart of the rubber stamp. In Noah's day, the eight believers (Noah, his wife, his three sons, and their wives) survived the flood because the ark in which they took refuge in protected them from God's judgment of the world. When the flood was over, they began a new life.

When it says that baptism "now saves us" it does not mean that the water has any saving properties. It refers to the underlying truth of baptism, which pictures the judgment Christ endured on the cross. He endured the judgment and triumphed over it just as the ark survived the flood and preserved those inside it. It is this truth that we as believers demonstrate when we are baptized. We publicly identify ourselves with God's condemnation of sin that Christ endured as our representative at Calvary. We also commit, as it were, to *staying* "dead to sin" and its influence over us, but we emerge from the baptismal waters to live victoriously over sin, empowered by the risen Christ.

Peter goes on to say that the purpose of baptism is "not the removal of the filth of the flesh." The water of baptism does not wash away a single sin. Rather, it is "the answer of a good conscience toward God." A "good conscience" can only be ours through the resurrection of Jesus Christ, which assures us of His triumph over sin and death. It is, therefore, ultimately, our own triumph.

Christ Is the Sovereign of the Universe (3:22)

Verse 22 is the climax to the section. The risen Christ has ascended to the "right hand of God, angels and authorities and powers having been made subject to Him." His ascension is described in Acts 1:6-11. The Lord Jesus Christ now has the place of highest honor and power. From that place He is available to suffering saints. He is the Sovereign of the whole universe, including the highest ranks of angelic spirit beings. When Christ rose from the dead He declared that all authority had been given to Him (Matt. 28:18). When He ascended He proclaimed His victory to the spirits "in prison." And now, at the right hand of the Father, He reigns.

These historical and doctrinal truths that give the "big picture" of what God has done would have comforted Peter's readers greatly, just as they should do for us today.

7

THE PILGRIM'S SUFFERING AND THE GLORY OF GOD (4:1-19)

The subject of the Christian in the world as a persecuted pilgrim is now more fully explained. In the light of Christ's triumph over sin, Peter appeals to his readers to prepare for their own "battle" as "Christian soldiers" but to expect to be victorious.

Have the Mindset of Christ (4:1)

Peter's appeal is linked to the victorious Christ who emerged from His suffering and death in wonderful triumph (v. 1). This is the fourth reference in the letter to Christ's suffering (1:11; 2:21; 3:18). The exhortation here identifies us with *His* attitude to the nature and consequences of sin. We too should condemn them by our attitude and actions. In so doing we will understand that when we stand against the world (which does not condemn sin, but rather glorifies it), we will suffer as He did (Rom. 8:12-17). Peter had heard the Lord say to all the disciples, "Yet because you are not of the world, but I chose you out of the world, therefore the world hates you. . . . If they persecuted Me, they will also persecute you" (John 15:19-20). So he admonishes us to arm ourselves with the mindset that Christ had.

"For he who has suffered in the flesh has ceased from sin" (v. 1b). The suffering believer who has counted himself dead to sin is a person who has already made the hard choice. He has made a clean break with sin in principle. He is no longer controlled by it. (This does not mean that he never sins; rather, that he does not practice sin as a way of life.) He has been morally strengthened by his decision. An Old Testament example of this moral strength is Daniel, who would not compromise when he knew that his enemies had plotted to have him thrown to the lions if he were caught praying. "He went home . . . with his windows open . . . he knelt down . . . and prayed" (Dan. 6:10). Compromise was out of the question for Daniel because he had long ago decided to obey God no matter the circumstances.

Live for the Will of God (4:2)

Peter tells us a second thing about the suffering believer. Not only is he no longer controlled by sin; he is controlled, instead, by the will of God. He has put his life under God's control, which ensures no relapse back to the old sinful ways. The phrase "the rest of his time" refers to the short period remaining to live on earth. As a pilgrim he always has his destination in view and the time it takes to get there. The mentally prepared pilgrim rejects being controlled by his own fleshly desires. Instead he accepts the principle of the will of God for the rest of his life on earth.

Do Not Return to Sinful Lifestyles (4:3)

One way Peter's pilgrim readers were to consciously condemn sin was to recognize that they had spent "enough" of their lives indulging the flesh. In verse 3 he lists six sins that characterized their past lifestyle in the pagan Gentile world. The sins revolve around sex, alcohol, and false religion, just as today where impurity in many forms, drunkenness, drug use, and false gods abound. Peter calls this godless lifestyle "the will of the Gentiles," in contrast to the God-honoring lifestyle in verse 2 lived according to "the will of God."

Take Comfort in Present Opposition (4:4)

The believers now find that their unsaved and former friends speak ill of them. The Christians' identification with Jesus Christ has influenced their lives to the degree that they "do not run with them in the same flood of dissipation." The expression "run with them" indicates the fast pace of their stampede for selfish pleasure. The Christians refuse to participate in the "dissipation," which can be defined as uncontrolled indulgence in seeking pleasure. It is the same word used in the parable Jesus taught of the prodigal (spendthrift) son who wasted his possessions in worldly pleasures (Luke 15:13). Jesus spoke about those who "loved darkness rather than light. . . .

For everyone practicing evil hates the light" (John 3:19-20). We can expect to be "judged" or criticized by unbelievers when we refuse to continue with them in sinful lifestyles, just as these believers were.

Take Comfort in Future Judgment (4:5-6)

In the end, however, the unbelieving persecutors of God's people will be the ones who are judged. "They will give an account to Him who is ready to judge the living and the dead" (v. 5). The Lord Jesus Christ is the Judge (John 5:22; 2 Tim. 4:1). That honor crowns His exalted position where authorities and powers have been made subject to Him (3:22). The "living and the dead" refers to unbelievers of all time. In one sense, unbelievers are already judged (John 3:18, 36). But the day will come when everyone who has not believed in God's Son will be judged once and for all. The Judge is "ready"; judgment *will* come. For those alive at the end of the tribulation it will be just prior to the millennium; for the dead unbelievers at that time, at the great white throne. What a different prospect is in view for the believer for whom salvation, not judgment, is "ready to be revealed" (1:5)!

The reminder of the certainty of coming judgment on the persecutors would have brought encouragement to these pilgrim believers. The righteous living of some believers was being "judged" and condemned by sinful men to the extent of being martyred for their faith. But their righteous living was being *vindicated* by God. His purpose was accomplished in them: the gospel had been preached to them, they had believed it, and they were now enjoying eternal life and peace with the Lord in heaven.

From unregenerate man's perspective, the death of believers might cause them to conclude that the dead Christians' faith had not accomplished much for them. They were, after all, now dead and in the grave. But they would be wrong—their life had not been futile and the grave is not final. The phrases "according to men in the flesh" and "according to God in the spirit" are contrasted sharply. Life in the realm of the flesh—this earthly life—is transient. Believers in heaven have entered fully into the realm of the spirit, which is forever. So there is great encouragement in knowing that a glorious future is in store for believers in Christ.

Be Ready! The End Is "At Hand" (4:7a)

In the first section of the chapter, Peter has alluded to the future in speaking of the believer living "the rest of his time . . . for the will of God" and then passing out of human life into heaven, the realm of the spirit. But what about believers who were still living? He assures them that the plan of God for them is unfolding rapidly and the end of all things is at hand. The "end of all things" refers to the completion of God's universal saving purpose. This will include the revelation of Jesus Christ in power and great glory (compare verse 13) and the establishment of peace on earth when He rules as the Messiah. Ultimately it includes the eternal state in the new heaven and new earth (2 Peter 3:10-13; Rev. 21:1).

The New Testament consistently teaches that the second coming of Christ should be in the conscious minds of God's people. Like the early believers, we are to be ready and waiting for His coming. The fact that nearly 2,000 years have passed does not invalidate it. We too look for the consummation of all things. It is only God's longsuffering that holds back Christ's return to reign.

Be Alert and Pray (4:7b)

When we live in the expectation of Christ's return we will pay attention to how we live. Peter mentions several Christian graces which ought to be evident in our lives. Note they are all in the realm of our relationship to "one another" in the church. How we treat and relate to other believers is very important to the Lord. When we live by these standards we will not need to be ashamed when we see Him.

First, we need clear and controlled thinking, which will prompt us to respond to every situation with prayer. He says, "Therefore be serious and watchful in your prayers" (v. 7). To "be serious" is to be sane, to evaluate situations correctly, and to think clearly. The word translated "watchful" is the same word as "sober" in 1:13 and refers to being in full control of our faculties. Two attitudes of mind lead us to effective prayer—clear thinking and controlled thinking. "Prayers" refer to prayers of all kinds, in all situations, while we wait for God to work out His purposes that will culminate in a new heaven and a new earth. As we carefully evaluate events in our personal lives, in the family of God, in the community, and in the world, only then can we pray effectively.

Love One Another (4:8)

The second grace needed in the light of the fact that the end of all things is at hand is love. Its importance is "above all things," which means that love for other Christians comes before everything else. This is now Peter's fourth reference to it (1:22; 2:17; 3:8). Its constant necessity is highlighted in the words, "Have fervent love for one another." The word-picture of a horse at full gallop illustrates the intensity of the word "fervent." Its mutual nature is stressed in the phrase "one another." As aliens in this hostile world we need the love of others in the body of Christ.

One reason for loving one another is that "love will cover a multitude of sins." Peter quotes from Proverbs 10:12: "Hatred stirs up strife, but love covers all sins." When we genuinely love one another we overlook and forgive many failings and weaknesses that otherwise we would expose. Love looks for the best construction in every situation. Without love, every act and word is liable to the worst interpretation through suspicion and misunderstanding. Roots of bitterness easily spring up, ". . . and by this many become defiled" (Heb. 12:15). To "cover" sins does not mean that we should either condone or approve them. But it does mean that the knowledge of such sin should not be spread any wider than is necessary for the biblical cleansing and restoration of the offender.

Be Hospitable (4:9)

The third of the Christian graces Peter addresses in this section is hospitality, which is a very practical expression of Christian love (v. 9) and refers to Christians practicing hospitality to one another in their homes. In Peter's day, believers met in homes, for they did not have church buildings, and there was a need to house traveling preachers. Also, as society was growing increasingly hostile to Christianity, believers who had become displaced needed housing. Note that the command is given to *all* the believers—not just those with more money and bigger homes. Evidently some were doing it unwillingly, so Peter told them to do it without complaint. Hospitality to others is kindness to the Lord Himself (Matt. 25:40). We should especially show hospitality to those who cannot pay us back in any way.

Exercise Your Gifts (4:10-11a)

The next grace mentioned is ministering to one another by using the gifts given to believers (v. 10). Note that each of us has received one or more gifts. The gifts may be spiritual gifts or natural gifts to be used as directed by the Spirit. Both kinds of gifts are to be employed in serving others; they are for our mutual edification (Rom. 12:6-8; 1 Cor. 12:7-11). God has entrusted them to us and we are responsible to be good stewards of them by using them to benefit other believers and building up the church. We become channels of blessing to others of God's "manifold" (literally, "multicolored") grace, which here means the diverse spiritual benefits others get when we serve them in using our gifts.

Two categories of good stewardship are given now—in speaking and in serving (v. 11). The "speaking" refers to all the gifts which employ speech activity, such as teaching, preaching, witnessing, and singing. When speaking, the "steward" of the gift is to "speak as the oracles of God." An oracle is an authoritative message from God. He should be convinced that what he has to say is a word from God for the occasion.

The second category of stewardship is "ministering" or serving. This is the same verb used in verse 10 and refers to forms of ministry other than speaking such as practical helps, giving, leading, and showing mercy. These gifts are to be used "with the ability which God supplies." They can only be used effectively with God's enabling, not in human strength or will. Good stewards will acknowledge what Jesus said to His disciples, ." . . without Me you can do nothing" (John 15:5).

The Goal of God's Glory (4:11b)

The section beginning in verse 7 ends with the goal of all Christian living, which is "that in all things God may be glorified through Jesus Christ." The goal of our prayers, love, hospitality, and ministry is that they result in God's name and reputation being honored. It echoes Paul's statement, "Whatever you do, do all to the glory of God" (1 Cor. 10:31). God's glory is accomplished "through Jesus Christ." Peter closes with a doxology, "to whom belong the glory and the dominion forever and ever. Amen." It is Peter's own response to the truth that God is indeed glorified through His Son.

The Glory of Suffering as a Christian (4:12-13)

Up to this point, Peter's comments about suffering have indicated that it was a possibility for some of his readers in a hostile world. Now he turns to others in different situations where persecution was actually happening. Peter is writing to many believers scattered over several provinces in many different circumstances. Some of them in those same provinces had faced violent opposition from the beginning, as we know from the New Testament record (Acts 13:50-52; 14:4-6, 19; 19:23-34).

Their persecution is described as a "fiery trial" to emphasize its intensity. This imagery is drawn from the refining of silver in a furnace, where it is heated to melting point in order to purify it. Christians are often called to endure the "fire" of persecution. We are not to be surprised or thrown off balance when it comes. Christians may suffer by losing their jobs, being treated abusively, being ostracized by relatives, or being boycotted in their business. God always has His purpose in it.

Instead of being surprised by fiery trials, we are to "rejoice to the extent that you partake of Christ's sufferings." If we boldly stand up for the Lord we should not expect to be treated better than He was. The world still hates the Lord Jesus Christ and will persecute those who are fully committed to Him (Matt. 10:24-25). But when we share His sufferings in this way we should rejoice, realizing that it is a privilege and an honor. It is a privilege now, and when His glory is ultimately revealed, it will be an honor. Our "joy" now will become "exceeding joy" then.

The Blessing of Suffering as a Christian (4:14-16)

We should view suffering for the name of Christ as more of a blessing than a hardship. The blessing is that the "Spirit of glory and of God rests upon you" (v. 14). Believers who suffer for His name will experience the Holy Spirit's fullness and presence in a special way. Read Psalm 69, a messianic psalm, for insights into the reproaches that Christ suffered from men, in particular, verses 7-12 and 19-21. We are in good company when we are "reproached for the name of Christ." The word "glory" suggests the imagery of the cloud of glory which rested on the tabernacle in Old Testament times. Now, the glory of His presence rests on the suffering believer. Christ's enemies may curse His name, but Christians who suffer for His name's sake bring Him glory.

The blessing is not given to every person who suffers. There is no glory to God when a believer is guilty of sin and rightly suffers for it. "Let none of you suffer as a murderer, a thief, an evildoer, or as a busybody in other people's matters" (v. 15). These four sins cover a broad spectrum; we would tend to not count meddling as serious as murder, but the principle is that a Christian who commits any of these sins and experiences their consequences brings shame on the name of their Savior.

To suffer as a "Christian," however, glorifies God. The word "Christian" is used in the Bible only here in verse 16 and in Acts 11:26 and Acts 26:28. When the term was first coined it was used in a derogatory sense; unbelievers looked on followers of Christ with disgust. The world may think that when a Christian suffers for witnessing or praying in public, the Christian would feel shame. But verse 16 says, "Let him not be ashamed, but let him glorify God in this matter." The Christians were to turn their suffering for Christ into an occasion for thanksgiving and praise to God. Peter himself had been whipped by Jewish leaders and emerged from this experience rejoicing that he was "counted worthy to suffer shame for His name" (Acts 5:41).

The Discipline of Suffering as a Christian (4:17-19)

Peter introduces one further consideration into the subject of Christian suffering, one that relates to the judgment of God. The "fire" they were experiencing was really the beginning of God's judgment. "For the time has come for judgment to begin at the house of God" (v. 17). The word used for "judgment" refers to an evaluation which may result in approval or discipline, just as the refining process does on silver, separating out any impurities so that the metal is fit to be made into something useful. Because God is holy, He cannot condone sin. It is appropriate for God to begin the process of judgment within the church during the present age.

The idea of beginning at the house of God is an allusion to Ezekiel 9:1-6. God showed Ezekiel through a hole in the wall of the temple that the leaders were practicing many abominable sins inside. Six executioners were sent forth to judge all the unfaithful in the land. They were to begin their work "in the sanctuary." In the same way, God has begun His corrective judgment in the church.

But there is another kind of judgment referred to in this passage. After the church is complete and has been caught up to heaven at the rapture,

God will begin to judge on earth those who have not obeyed the gospel (during the tribulation). Peter's point is that if God is severe with His own household (the redeemed), how much more terrible it will be for those who die in their sins!

In verse 18 Peter poses a second question along the same line of thought, taken from Proverbs 11:31: "If the righteous one is scarcely saved, where will the ungodly and the sinner appear?" The "righteous" is the saved person, who can never lose his eternal life. But even *he* is saved with difficulty—that is, he must pass through hard circumstances and under the disciplinary hand of his heavenly Father. The aspect of salvation in this context refers to the sanctification process we experience in this earthly life. Paul said in Acts 14:22 that "we must through many tribulations enter the kingdom of God." If this is how it is for the "righteous," how will it then be for the ungodly?

In conclusion, Peter encourages "those who suffer according to the will of God [to] commit their souls to Him in doing good, as to a faithful Creator" (v. 19). Suffering according to God's will includes those sufferings which result from faithful witnessing and righteous living. It does not include suffering which results from foolish choices or ungodly living. Suffering saints should turn themselves over to God. He created us physically and spiritually and knows best how to care for us. The term "Creator" also indicates His power and His broad, eternal purposes. This puts temporary suffering in proper perspective.

8

THE PILGRIM SHEPHERDS AND THEIR FLOCKS (5:1-14)

The final chapter in Peter's first letter contains advice to the elders of the widely scattered churches. Leading a church under severe pressure from the world presented its own set of problems. These elders of the local churches are called shepherds, and their work is therefore compared to looking after sheep which are, by nature, fearful and insecure when under stress. Peter's counsel to the shepherds in the first section is followed by his counsel to the "flocks" under their charge.

Peter Counsels the Church Elders (5:1-4)

The chapter opens, "The elders who are among you I exhort." Peter specifically addresses the elders who were "among" the churches. Each church had a group of elders as its official leaders. The plurality of elders is the consistent pattern for the New Testament church (Acts 14:23; 20:17; 1 Thess. 5:12; Phil. 1:1). The faithfulness and character of these men is vital, especially in times of persecution.

There is a connection between Peter's exhortation to the elders and the previous chapter which does not show up in our text. Most Greek manuscripts begin with "therefore," referring back to the judgment that begins in the house of God (4:17). When God purifies His church He must begin with the leaders, so Peter begins with advice to the elders of these local congregations. Leadership is important to the spiritual health of a local church. It may well be that Peter still has in mind the Old Testament passage already referred to in 1 Peter 4:17 which reads, "So they began with the elders who were before the temple" (Ezek. 9:6). Correction should always begin with the leadership.

Peter's Own Example (v. 1)

Peter describes himself in three ways which at first may surprise us. First, he calls himself a "fellow-elder." The well known apostle identifies himself with these elders. He does not place himself above them or claim any special office just because He had been a close companion of the Lord Jesus or because he was an apostle. People who would make Peter the head of the church find no support here. Peter is happy to be an example to them before he asks them to be examples to others (v. 3).

The second way he describes himself is "a witness of the sufferings of Christ." Peter draws attention to this even though he had failed miserably during the period when Christ's sufferings reached their climax. The recollection of it would have been painful to him. In Gethsemane he fell asleep while Jesus was in agony anticipating His crucifixion. At the trials, while witnessing Jesus being abused, he vehemently denied being His disciple. The Bible does not record Peter being present at Christ's crucifixion, but it is possible that he observed it from a safe distance. He had failed under pressure, and that is the reason he brings it up here. His life was living proof that restoration is possible after failure and discipline. He writes to elders who themselves might fail—what comfort they could take from Peter! Even though he had actually witnessed the sufferings of Christ and failed, he was now restored and serving well. They too could be encouraged to endure hardship at the risk of failure. They too could admit their failings instead of pretending to be perfect.

The third thing about himself that Peter describes is that he is "a partaker of the glory that will be revealed." He is deeply impressed that the Lord Jesus who suffered for him on the cross would soon share His glory with him. Peter was only a witness of those sufferings, and a poor one at that. But Peter will partake in Christ's glory when it is unveiled before the world. With this wonderful hope in view, he can "exhort" these elders to continue to steadfastly serve the Lord. They too will share in Christ's glory.

This is the third time in the letter that both the suffering and the glory of Christ have been mentioned together. The suffering and the glory of Christ were the great themes of the Old Testament prophets (1:11). They were to be the cause for rejoicing for believers who were suffering as He suffered (4:13). And here in this passage they give elders under pressure the stimulation to continue faithfully to shepherd the flocks under their care.

The Duty of Shepherds (v. 2a)

The elders' duty is simply stated: "Shepherd the flock of God." They must first be conscious that their local congregation does not belong to them, it belongs to God and they are merely its caretakers—a solemn responsibility. They are to "*shepherd* the flock," meaning to tend as a shepherd. The Lord Jesus Himself commanded Peter, "Tend My sheep" (John 21:16). In that context, Peter had emerged from his own failure and was charged with both feeding and tending (two different words) the Lord's sheep. The tending, used here in verse 2, includes leading, restoring, and disciplining, as well as feeding. The task of shepherds in the local assembly is to carefully tend the flock. Paul used the same word when he instructed the elders in Ephesus to "shepherd the church of God which He [Christ] purchased with His own blood" (Acts 20:28).

The shepherds should not be absentee shepherds; they are to be "among" them or around them. It is important to *be* there, actively working with the flock. They are also to be "serving as overseers," meaning they were to "watch over" them. The word is translated "bishop" in 1 Timothy 3:1-2 and in Titus 1:7. Note, however, that the very terms over which Christian denominations have divided regarding church government are all used in 1 Peter 5:1-2 of the same group of leaders in every local church—elders / presbyters, shepherds / pastors, overseers / bishops. No official difference between elders, bishops, and pastors is warranted in the New Testament; the terms are used interchangeably (Acts 20:17-28).

The Motives of Shepherds (vv. 2b-3)

In exercising their shepherding duty, Peter gives advice about three areas to do with their own personal motives for doing so. In avoiding three common temptations in their work, they should have three virtuous motives. First, they are to shepherd "not by compulsion but willingly." The temptation is to occupy the office because "someone has to do it" or because pressure is brought to bear on them. Rather, they should have a healthy *spiritual* desire for the work of shepherding which will result in diligence and excellence in their service.

The second instruction is, "not for dishonest gain but eagerly," in other words, not for material advantage. Money should never be a motive. This does not mean that elders giving all or much of their time to the work of the local church should not be supported financially (1 Tim. 5:18). It means that the men who take up this ministry should not be motivated by material profit. Instead, they should be motivated by spiritual desires.

The third counsel Peter gives relates to "being lords over those entrusted to you." The misuse of authority by those greedy for power is always a danger and snare to leaders. Elders should not govern by intimidating or threatening the congregation or by using controlling tactics. Diotrephes was that kind of a leader; he loved power and recognition (3 John 9-10). God entrusts His sheep to the care of elders and they are therefore responsible to Him to do it by loving—not lording over—the sheep. The way to avoid lording over the church is to lead by "being examples to the flock." Elders are to be models of humility and godliness that the people can imitate. Peter has emphasized three keys to effective leadership in the local church: willingness, eagerness, and godliness.

The Reward for Shepherds (v. 4)

Faithful elders should look beyond the present world for any reward. "And when the Chief Shepherd appears, you will receive the crown of glory that does not fade away." It is fitting that Christ is called the Chief Shepherd here in relation to the elders who are shepherds of local churches. He is also called the Good Shepherd, who laid down His life *for* the sheep (John 10:11), and the Great Shepherd, who is working out His purposes *in* all the sheep (Heb. 13:20). In this passage, Christ is the Chief Shepherd who will reward the work of the under-shepherds when He appears (literally, "is made visible") at His coming. Faithful elders will receive a crown of glory.

The prospect of a crown of glory in heaven was intended to motivate faithfulness in elders on earth. Crowns, or wreaths made of leaves or flowers, were given to winners in athletic contests in those days to recognize their achievement. They are not to be confused with the crowns (diadems) that kings wear which are symbols of their office. These wreaths would have soon wilted and died. In contrast, the crown for faithful shepherding in the church will *not* fade away. We do not know the exact nature of these crowns, nor is it profitable to speculate, but we do know that what they indicate of service to the Lord on earth is important to Him. The Lord Jesus delights to recognize faithful service with His commendation, "Well done." Other crowns mentioned in the Bible are: an "imperishable crown" (1 Cor. 9:25); a "crown of rejoicing" (1 Thess. 2:19); a "crown of righteousness" (2 Tim. 4:8); and a "crown of life" (James 1:12; Rev. 2:10).

Peter Counsels the Local Flocks (5:5-9)

The subject now turns from the shepherding of the elders to the following of the flock. Peter speaks first to the "younger people" and then appeals to the whole assembly for humility and watchfulness.

Obey Your Shepherds (v. 5)

Younger people, whether younger in age or younger in the faith, should submit to their elders, just as citizens should submit to government (2:13), employees to employers (2:18), and wives to husbands (3:1). The elders' spiritual experience and knowledge of the Scriptures qualifies them to lead. The younger are exhorted to be submissive—to place themselves under the authority of their spiritual leaders. The word "younger" may have been deliberately used instead of a more inclusive word because the young often need to be reminded to be humble and submissive.

Humble Yourselves (vv. 5-6)

A new line of thought begins here concerning all interpersonal relationships in the fellowship of the local church. "Yes, all of you be submissive to one another, and be clothed with humility." The attitude of everyone in the church toward everyone else is to come from a humble heart and mind. We should take delight in thinking of others first and in serving them gladly. It is the opposite of the self-serving attitude that is so prevalent in this world that is obsessed with pleasing self.

Peter describes humility using the imagery of clothing that has to be put on. Humility is not being conveyed as beautiful clothing here. A better picture is that of a Roman slave tying on the apron which marked him out as slave. Moffatt translates this phrase, "Put on the ap:on of humility," which captures the idea well. We are to have the mind of the Lord Jesus Christ who took "the form of a bondservant" (Phil. 2:5-7). When He washed the feet of the disciples, doing a servant's work, He told them, "I have given you an example, that you should do as I have done to you" (John 13:15). There would be fewer problems in our local congregations if all the believers practiced the virtue of humility, yet it remains one of the rarest of all virtues.

The subject of humbling ourselves toward one another is expanded to include our humility before God. The need for humility is reinforced by a quote from the Greek Old Testament: "God resists the proud, but gives grace to the humble" (v. 5; Prov. 3:34; see also James 4:6). The consistent testimony of Scripture is that God condemns pride (see, for example, 2 Chronicles 26:16-21; Isaiah 14:12-15; Daniel 4:28-37). But when people of lowly mind acknowledge their dependence on Him, He bestows His grace and favor on them (Isa. 57:15; 66:2).

To humble ourselves before God is to accept the circumstances we are in as being His providence, even though they may include "fiery trials" (4:12). The "mighty hand of God" is a familiar Old Testament expression which refers to God's irresistible actions in human affairs. In almost every reference, He is seen acting for His own people (see Deut. 5:15). This is the only use of the phrase in the New Testament. Under God's "mighty hand" we can humble ourselves with confidence, because in due time God will exalt us, which is probably when Christ comes again.

Cast Your Anxiety on God (v. 7)

"Casting all your care upon Him, for He cares for you." This favorite verse of many believers is directly linked with the previous command to humble ourselves. Once again Peter quotes from the Greek New Testament, this time Psalm 55:22. Part of being truly humble-minded is recognizing our inability to solve our own problems ("care"). As a result, we take those problems to the Lord. Worry is the modern word for these cares. Worry is sin because it leaves God out of the situation. Casting our worries onto God is a spiritual exercise of trusting Him.

The "casting" describes a definite act of handing over. We should throw on God all burdens that cause any anxiety. To keep them is to trust in our own ability or strength to handle them. We are to cast the worrisome burdens on Him because "He cares for [us]." This word "care" is a different one to the first word also translated "care." Everything that creates anxiety to us is of great concern to Him. God the Father is a caring God who faithfully feeds the birds and clothes the lilies and is even more concerned about His own people (Matt. 6:25-34). This verse would have comforted any believers to whom Peter was writing who were burdened with great concerns about living in a world that did not provide for their needs.

Beware of Satan's Threats (vv. 8-9)

The subject of Peter's counsel now moves from our spiritual rest in God who cares for us to spiritual watchfulness against attack from the enemy. The pilgrim road passes through enemy territory; let the pilgrim beware! Peter exhorts his readers to "be sober" for the third time. First, be sober by correctly assessing this world from a biblical perspective (1:13). Second, be sober in prayer in view of the nearness of the end (4:7). Third, be sober so you can watch out for your powerful enemy (5:8). Spiritual sobriety is clear, controlled thinking. Anxiety, which focuses on self, can cloud our spiritual concentration and therefore dull our sense of the enemy's presence and power.

"Be vigilant" is an exhortation to be watchful—to be spiritually and morally alert to the attacks of the evil one. Peter would vividly remember the Lord using this word in the Garden of Gethsemane when He found the disciples asleep and said to him, "What, could you not watch with Me one hour?" (Matt. 26:40). The elders at Ephesus were reminded of the danger of "wolves" disturbing the flock. Paul warned them to "therefore watch" (Acts 20:31).

The enemy is identified as "your adversary the devil." The term "adversary," which is usually used of an opponent in a lawsuit (Matt. 5:25), refers more generally to the enemy of our souls, Satan. The Greek equivalent of "Satan" is "devil," the term used for him thirty-two times in the New Testament. Jesus Himself was tempted by the devil in the wilderness (Matt. 4:1-11). The devil commands a host of fallen angels in his crusade to thwart the purposes of God on earth. In the New Testament the devil and his demonic hosts are always seen opposing the gospel and often demonstrating violent, irrational behavior.

Satan is described here as a "roaring lion." Lions are known to be cunning predators that pounce on unsuspecting prey. The use of the adjective "roaring," however, emphasizes in this context the *ferocity* and threatening nature of a lion. Like frightened sheep, Peter's audience was in danger of succumbing to fear of persecution. The word "devour" means to swallow, or gulp down. Satan cannot destroy a believer (as in snatching away his eternal salvation), but he can overwhelm him and make him an ineffectual witness for Christ by tempting him to give up his stand for Christ out of fear of being persecuted. We should not, however, cower in dread when the devil roars. We should "resist him" by taking a solid stand against him "steadfast in the faith," that is, with a firm, personal confidence that "He who is in you is greater than he who is in the world" (1 John 4:4). James tells us, "Resist the devil and he will flee from you" (James 4:7). The main weapons we are told to use in resisting the devil are prayer and the "sword of the Spirit, the word of God" (Eph. 6:16-17).

If we are resisting the devil we are encouraged when we understand that our suffering is not unique: "Knowing that the same sufferings are experienced by your brotherhood in the world" (v. 9). Suffering is a necessary part of the Christian life while we are in a world that rejects Christ. Jesus told His disciples, "In the world you will have tribulation; but be of good cheer, I have overcome the world" (John 16:33).

Peter Reassures the Sufferers (5:10-11)

The suffering of the believer is not an end in itself, as Peter has said before. It may seem difficult, but it will not last long. Christians can rest in the fact that the God with the "mighty hand" (v. 6) is "the God of all grace" (v. 10). He has dealt with us in grace, or unmerited favor, in saving us. Now, in our trials, He provides "grace" of a different kind—divine help and strength for every need. If God has "*called*" us to His eternal glory," so He will not fail to bring us there. "After you have suffered a while" is the final reference to a major theme of this letter. The pilgrim's temporary suffering is contrasted to the eternal glory ahead. Peter prays a blessing on his readers citing four things he is confident that God will do for them to keep them secure while suffering and waiting to be called home.

First, He will "perfect"—that is, make fully complete or mature. Jesus used the word "perfect" in this way when He said, "Everyone who is perfectly trained will be like his teacher" (Luke 6:40). Second, He will "establish," which means He will make sure we do not totter and fall. Third, He will "strengthen" us. Fourth, He will "settle" us, He will place us on a solid foundation, which in this context would be the Lord Himself and His Word. Peter then bursts into a short doxology of praise: "To Him be the glory and the dominion forever and ever. Amen."

Peter Concludes His Letter (5:12-14)

Silvanus was the one to whom Paul dictated the letter. He is the same person known as Silas who accompanied Paul on the second missionary journey through Macedonia (Acts 15:40-17:15). He is mentioned three more times as Silvanus in Paul's epistles. Paul commends Silvanus to the churches as "our faithful brother."

Peter mentions the double thrust he had in writing to them: "exhorting and testifying that this is the true grace of God in which you stand" (v. 12).

Peter has been earnestly persuading them that they should trust God during the times of persecution. He has also been testifying to the reality of the message of grace. Recall the great passages that describe the sufferings of Christ and the glories to follow. He confirms to them the truth of the wonderful work of Christ in His death and resurrection.

"She who is in Babylon, elect together with you, greets you" (v. 13). Commentators have wrestled with the meaning of this verse. It is easiest to understand "she" as a reference to the local church in Babylon, the literal city on the Euphrates River. All other geographical references in 1 Peter are actual places. Some have suggested it is a cryptic reference to the city of Rome, but this seems unlikely. The reference to "Mark my son" is probably to John Mark, the author of the Gospel of Mark, who may well have been Peter's spiritual son. Paul referred to Timothy in the same way (1 Tim. 1:2, 18).

The "kiss of love" with which they were to greet one another was a display of affection, a kiss on the cheek, and a common form of greeting (Rom. 16:16; 1 Cor. 16:20; Luke 7:45). Peter closes his letter with a benediction of peace. How fitting that pilgrims in a turbulent world should be blessed with true peace!